SPECIAL EDITION

2007 Salem Manager's Meeting

CLASSIC HYMN STORIES

Inspiring Stories Behind Our Best-loved Hymns

LOUIS F. BENSON

Originally Published in 1903

Introduction

Louis Fitzgerald Benson left a successful law practice in 1877 to devote his life to the study of hymns. By the early 1900's he was considered the country's leading authority in hymnology and he possessed the largest library of hymnals ever assembled—more than 9,000 volumes (the entire library now resides at the Princeton Seminary Library).

Everywhere he went he spoke of how hymns had the power to stir and restore the soul. Churches across America knew Benson for his love and devotion to God through hymns. "Do you know what a hymn is?" he wrote. "It is singing to the praise of God. If you praise God and do not sing, you utter no hymn. If you praise anything which does not pertain to the praise of God—though in singing you praise, you utter no hymn. A hymn then contains these three things: song, and praise, and that of God."

Benson wrote this particular book in 1903. It was originally entitled A Study of Familiar Hymns, and it gives a unique "behind the scenes" stories of hymns and their authors. This book has been out-of-print for generations. We are honored to bring it back and to make it available once again to a new generation, using revolutionary digital and print-on-demand publishing technologies. This book is reprinted in it's original format; it has not been edited for the use of contemporary spelling and grammar.

—Xulon Press, a part of Salem Communications

Table of Contents

I

O LITTLE TOWN OF BETHLEHEM

THE TEXT OF THE HYMN

1   O little town of Bethlehem,
         How still we see thee lie;
     Above thy deep and dreamless sleep
         The silent stars go by:
     Yet in they dark streets shineth
         The everlasting Light;
     The hopes and fears of all the years
         Are met in thee to-night.

2   For Christ is born of Mary;
         And gathered all above,
     While mortals sleep, the angels keep
         Their watch of wondering love.
     O morning stars, together
         Proclaim the holy birth;
     And praises sing to God the King,
         And peace to men on earth.

3   How silently, how silently,
         The wondrous gift is given!
     So God imparts to human hearts
         The blessings of His heaven.
     Nor ear may hear His coming,
         But in this world of sin,
     Where meek souls will receive Him still,
         The dear Christ enters in.

4   O holy Child of Bethlehem,
    Descend to us, we pray;
   Cast out our sin, and enter in,
    Be born in us to-day.
   We hear the Christmas angels
    The great glad tidings tell;
   O come to us, abide with us,
    Our Lord Emmanuel

Rev. Phillips Brooks, 1868

NOTE.–Four verses of the five as originally written (see under "Some Points for Discussion"). This text agrees with the author's manuscript. That issued by Bishop Brook's publishers in "illuminated" style was inaccurate.

THE STORY OF THE HYMN

It was the sight of Bethlehem itself, one feels very sure, that gave Phillips Brooks the impulse to write this hymn. He was then rector of the Church of Holy Trinity, in Philadelphia, and had spent a year's vacation traveling in Europe and the East. "After an early dinner, we took our horses and rode to Bethlehem," so he wrote home in Christmas week of 1865. "It was only about two hours when we came to the town, situated on an eastern ridge of a range of hills, surrounded by its terraced gardens. It is a good-looking town, better built than any other we have seen in Palestine ... Before dark, we rode out of town to the field where they say the shepherds saw the star. It is a fenced piece of ground with a cave in it (all the Holy Places are caves here), in which, strangely enough, they put the shepherds. The story is absurd, but somewhere in those fields we rode through the shepherds must have been ... As we passed, the shepherds were still 'keeping watch over their flocks,' "or leading them home to fold." Mr. Brooks returned in September, 1866, and it must have been while meditating at home over what he had seen that the carol took shape in his mind. The late Dr. Arthur Brooks assured the writer that it was not written until 1868.

Its history as a hymn begins then, and a considerable share of the credit for its popularity must be given to Mr. Redner, at that time organist of the church, superintendent of its mission, and teacher in the church school. The place of the carol in the books is now established, and new tunes have been and will be written for it. But it is safe to say that Mr. Redner's music was what carried the carol into notice and popularity. If the tune to which it was suns at that service had been unsuccessful, it is unlikely that the carol would have been reprinted or heard again, at least during Bishop Brooks' life.

With this view of the case it seemed to present writer well worth while that an account, as circumstantial as possible, of the genesis of the hymn and tune should be secured from the one man living who knows it. And standing over Mr. Redner in his Walnut Street office in Philadelphia one winter afternoon, waving aside the modest protests and gently prodding the reluctance of that genial composer, he was happy in obtaining the following written statement of the circumstances: "As Christmas of 1868 approached, Mr. Brooks told me that he had written a simple little carol for the Christmas Sunday-school service, and he asked me to write the tune to it. The simple music was written in great haste and under great pressure. We were to practice it on the following Sunday. Mr. Brooks came to me on Friday, and said, 'Redner, have you ground out that music yet to "O Little Town of Bethlehem"?' I replied, 'No,' but that he should have it by Sunday. On Saturday night previous my brain was all confused bout the tune. I thought more about my Sunday-school lesson than I did bout the music. But I was roused from sleep late in the night hearing an angel-strain whispering in my ear, and seizing a piece of music paper I jotted down the treble of the tune as we now have it, and on Sunday morning before going to church I filled in the harmony. Neither Mr. Brooks nor I ever thought the carol or the music to it would live beyond that Christmas of 1868.

"My recollection is that Richard McCauley, who then had a book-store on Chestnut Street west of Thirteenth Street, printed it on leaflets for sale. Rev. Dr. Huntington, rector of All Saints' Church, Worcester, Mass., asked permission to print it in his Sunday-school hymn and

11

tune book, called *The Church Porch*, and it was he who christened the music 'Saint Louis.'"

The date of Dr. Huntington's book, 1874, does not imply a very prompt recognition of the merits of the carol even as available for use in Sunday-school. Nor does its appearance in that book imply that the carol passed at that date into general use in Sunday-schools. But gradually it became familiar in those connected with the Protestant Episcopal Church. By the year 1890 it had begun to make its appearance in hymnals intended for use in church worship. In 1892 (some twenty-four years after its first appearance) Bishop Brooks's carol was given a place as a church hymn in the official hymnal of his own denomination. This occasioned the composition of new tunes to its words for rival musical editions of that book, and also drew attention afresh to the earlier tune of Mr. Redner. It seems, too, to have settled the status of the hymn, recent editors being as reluctant to omit the hymn as their predecessors had been to recognize it.

There is, however, nothing unusual or surprising in this delay in admitting the carol into the church hymnals. Almost all hymns undergo such a period of probation before they obtain recognition; and it is for the best interests of hymnody that they should. In this particular case there was an especial reason for delay. There had to be a certain change in the standards by which hymns are judged before a carol such as this could be esteemed suitable for church use. In 1868, it is likely, not even its author would have seriously considered it in such a connection.

THE AUTHOR OF THE HYMN

Phillips Brooks was born in Boston, December 13th, 1835. He came of a long line of Puritan ancestors, many of whom had been Congregational clergyman. His parents became connected with the Episcopal Church, and he was reared in the strict ways of the Evangelical wing of that Church. He had the typical Boston education, the Latin School and then Harvard, from which he was graduated in 1855. He was then for a few months a teacher in the Latin School, but there he had the humiliating experience of complete failure. He soon decided to enter the ministry, and studied at Alexandria Seminary, in Virginia. In 1859 he became rector of a small church in Philadelphia. Here his sermons attracted much attention, and in 1861 he was called to be rector of the Church of the Holy Trinity, in that same city.

In that position he remained until 1869, when his own leanings toward his native town and the urgency of repeated calls from there led him to accept the rectorship of Trinity Church, Boston. The congregation built for him the great church in the Back Bay, and there he exercised that wonderful ministry with which we all are familiar. In 1891 he was elected bishop of his Church in Massachusetts, and after some controversy, occasioned by his broad views in church matters, his election was confirmed and he was consecrated. But this position he was not to fill for long. The strain of the great work he had been doing had undermined even his giant strength, and after a short sickness he passed away on January 23rd, 1893.

Bishop Brooks was the most famous preacher and the most widely-loved clergyman of his time. The shock of his death was felt in every branch of the Church throughout the land, for while many disagreed with his opinions, none who knew him in his work could withhold their admiration. The word that seems best to describe him is "great". He was great in his physical proportions, great in the endowments of genius, great in the power to work, extraordinarily great in his personal influence over men, greatest of all in the moral elevation of his character and his ever-deepening spirit of consecration to Christ's service.

The connection of one so great with hymnody as the writer of a few simple carols intended for children seems at first a little incongruous. But after reading his biography, and understanding the man's nature, one feels rather that nothing he ever did was more characteristic of him. It now appears that verse-writing was even a regular habit with him, probably as a relief to feelings his intensely reserved nature could express in no other way. And he not only loved children dearly, but liked to be their comrade and to get down on the nursery floor and romp with them. His own heart was like a child's, and he wrote

Christmas and Easter carols because he entered into those festivals with a child's enthusiasm and joy.

But there is another point of connection between Bishop Brooks and hymnody which must not be passed over. Its disclosure was to many one of the surprises of that wonderful biography of his friend by Dr. Allen. And that connection is the fact that his own mind and heart were stored with hymns, to such an extent and in such a way that they were one of the real influences of his life.

In one of the letters "the father regrets that Phillips could not have been with the family on the last Sunday evening when the boys recited hymns. This was a beautiful custom, which called from each one of the children the learning of a new hymn every Sunday, and its recital before the assembled family. In a little book, carefully kept by the father, there was a record of the hymns each child had learned, beginning with William, who had the advantage of age, and had learned the greatest number, followed by Phillips, who came next, and the record tapering down until John is reached, with a comparatively small number at his disposal. Most of them were from the old edition of the Prayer Book, then bound up with a metrical selection of Psalms and a collection of two hundred twelve hymns." "But there were others. When Phillips went to college there were some two hundred that he could repeat. They constituted part of his religious furniture, or the soil whence grew much that cannot now be traced. He never forgot them." Again his biographer remarks: "These hymns Phillips carried in his mind as so much mental and spiritual furniture, or as germs of thought; they often reappeared in his sermons, as he became aware of some deeper meaning in the old familiar lines." Once more the biographer recurs to the subject; this time to speak of "the language of sacred hymns learned in childhood and forever ringing in his ears," as one of the channels through which "he had felt the touch of Christ."

II

STAND UP, STAND UP FOR JESUS

THE TEXT OF THE HYMN

1   Stand up, stand up for Jesus,
        Ye soldiers of the cross;
Lift high His royal banner,
        It must not suffer loss:
From victory unto victory
        His army He shall lead,
Till every foe is vanquished,
        And Christ is Lord indeed.

2   Stand up, stand up for Jesus,
        The trumpet call obey;
Forth to the might conflict
        In this His glorious day:
Ye that are men now serve Him
        Against unnumbered foes;
Let courage rise with danger,
        And strength to strength oppose.

3   Stand up, stand up for Jesus,
        Stand in His strength alone;
The arm of flesh will fail you,
        Ye dare not trust your own:
Put on the gospel armor,
        Each piece put on with prayer;
Where duty calls, or danger,
        Be never wanting there.

4   Stand up, stand up for Jesus,
   The strife will not be long;
  This day the noise of battle,
   The next the victor's song:
  To him that overcometh
   A crown of life shall be;
  He with the King of Glory
   Shall reign eternally.

          Rev. George Duffield, 1858

NOTE.–Four verses of the original six. The text is taken from a leaflet printed by the author in 1883.

THE STORY OF THE HYMN

Very few hymns have had so pathetic an origin as this. Its author, the Rev. George Duffield, was a pastor in Philadelphia during the great revival of the winter of 1857 and the spring of 1858, which centred about the Noonday Prayer Meetings in Jayne's Hall, under the charge of the Young Men's Christian Association.

The real leader of the movement was a young Episcopalian clergyman, Dudley A. Tyng. Though not yet thirty years old, he was well known for his stand for interdenominational fellowship and for the fervor of his evangelical zeal. In Philadelphia, at the time, he was especially before the public eye, having but lately, after a contest with his vestry, precipitated by a sermon in opposition to slave-holding, been compelled to retire from the rectorship of the Church of the Epiphany. He had gone forth with those sympathizing with him, and preached in a public hall, establishing there the Church of the Covenant. The band of clergymen of various denominations gathered about him was united not only by zeal in carrying on "The Work of God in Philadelphia," but also in admiration and affection for Mr. .Tyng; and not the less so for their general feeling that "he had been persecuted." Among those helpers was Mr. Duffield, a deeply attached friend, who thought Mr. Tyng "one of the most noblest, bravest, manliest men I ever met."

Athwart this fellowship and common work came the tragic interruption of Mr. Tyng's death. On Tuesday, April 13th, 1858, he went from the study of his country home to the barn floor where a mule was at work treading a machine for shelling corn. As he patted the animal on the neck the sleeve of his study-gown became caught in the cogs of the wheel, wrenching and lacerating his arm, from the neck down, in a dreadful manner. It seems that mortification set in. In any event amputation, performed on the Saturday following, did no more than postpone the end. Mr. Tyng died on Monday, April 19th, 1858.

Early that morning, it being perceived that he was sinking, he was asked if he had any messages to send, among others, to the band of clergymen so devoted to him and the work. When able to rouse himself sufficiently, he responded with a short message, beginning with the words: "Tell them, 'Let us all stand up for Jesus'." It is evident that thee words especially touched the already aroused feelings of his fellow-workers, Bishop MacIlvaine and the Rev. John Chambers quoted them at the funerals as their friend's dying message. At one of the Jayne's Hall meetings a poem was read from the platform by the Rev. Thomas H. Stockton, beginning:

> "Stand up for Jesus! Strengthen'd by His hand,
> Even I, though young, have ventured thus to stand;
> But, soon cut down, as maim'd and faint I lie,
> Hear, O my friends, the charge with which I die –
> Stand up for Jesus!"

And the Rev. Kingston Goddard, preaching to a great throng on the day after Mr. Tyng's death, remarked: "I conceive that the whole of my brother's teaching is contained in that grand and noble expression of heroism and devotion and that fell from his lips in his dying hour – '*Stand up for Jesus!*'"

Mr. Duffield had been present at these services, but, with his own feelings deeply stirred by his friend's tragic death, perhaps hardly needed such incentives to quicken the appeal of that dying message to his heart. On the Sunday following, he preached to his own people

17

from Ephesians vi. 14, and read as the concluding exhortation of the sermon the verses of his now famous hymn, into which he had wrought the message of his friend.

The superintendent of his Sunday-school, Mr. Benedict D. Stewart, had them printed on a fly leaf, they were copied by religious papers; they appeared in *The Sabbath Hymn Book* (Congregational) that same year, and in the Supplement to *The Church Psalmist* (Presbyterian) in the next y ear. The hymn became a favorite of the soldiers during the Civil War, and is now sung in churches and Sundays-schools all over the land and in many foreign countries.

Long afterwards (in 1883) Dr. Duffield printed a leaflet containing his preferred text of the hymn, and also his recollections of its origin. This has been often quoted from, and forms the familiar history of the hymn. Dr. Duffield's memory had retained its hold upon so much of the events as directly concerned himself, but it is plain that other dates and circumstances had become somewhat dimmed with the lapse of years. And the present writer has not hesitated to supplement and correct these recollections in the light of facts disclosed in the Memorial Volume published in the year of Mr. Tyng's death, and especially in the touching Memorial Sermon of Mr. Tyng's father (Stephen H. Tyng, D.D.), who was present during the closing days of his son's life.

"A cob of corn from that 'threshing floor,'" we are told by Dr. Duffield's son, in 1885, "has ever since hung on the study-wall of the author of the hymn." The hymn itself seems to echo the voice of his friend: "Tell them, 'Let us all stand up for Jesus,'" with his other words to those about him soon following, "Sing! Sing! Can you not sing?"

THE AUTHOR OF THE HYMN

In the ministry of the American Presbyterian Church there have been three distinguished men named George Duffield. The first (1732-1790) was a patriot and chaplain in the Revolutionary army. His grandson, the second George Duffield (1796-1868), was a successful pastor at Carlisle, Philadelphia, and other places, and an able theologian, whose work on Regeneration met with the disapproval of his Presbytery. It was his son, the third George Duffield, who was the author of this hymn. "The author is not his father, Rev. George Duffield, D.D., the Patriarch of Michigan," he found occasion to say after his hymn had become famous while his personality seemed obscured. "Neither is he his son, Rev. Samuel W. Duffield, ... now pastor of the Westminster Church, Bloomfield, N.J. [He] has not yet lost his identity, and claims to be his own individual self."

He was born at Carlisle, Pennsylvania, in 1818, was graduated from Yale College in 1837, and from Union Theological Seminary in 1840. In the same year he married, was ordained, and installed pastor of the Fifth Presbyterian Church in Brooklyn, where he remained seven years. It was as pastor and preacher, rather than as scholar or man of letters, that Dr. Duffield spent his life. After leaving Brooklyn he was pastor of the First Church of Bloomfield, New Jersey, for four years. In 1851 he broke off a happy pastorate there to accept the call of the Central Presbyterian Church of the Northern Liberties, Philadelphia, with the expectation of dinging in the great city an enlarged opportunity for usefulness. It seems quite certain that if he had not gone to Philadelphia we should never have had the hymn so closely connected with his experiences there. But to him, at the time, it must have seemed as though his going had been the mistake of his professional life. He found a mortgaged church building unfortunately located in a neighborhood from which the population was moving westward, a congregation reduced in numbers, disheartened, and unable to meet its financial obligations. Dr. Duffield's Philadelphia pastorate was not wanting in spiritual results, but with the conditions threatening the continued life of his church he was not able to cope. Year by year the congregation grew less in numbers and resources. Dr. Duffield, however, held on until 1861, when he resigned his pastorate. His subsequent pastorates were of a less conspicuous character, - at Adrian, Michigan, for four years, at Galesburg, Illinois, for an equal period, and then at Saginaw City, Michigan.

His active service covered more than forty years. Dr. Duffield's last years were lived in Bloomfield, with his son. The son, himself a poet, always recalled with pride that his hand had made the first "fair copy" of his father's hymn for the press, and those who saw father and son together at Bloomfield, still speak of the reverence and love with which that same hand supported the father's failing steps. But the son was first called, and it was more than a year before the father followed him. Dr. Duffield died at Bloomfield on July 6th, 1888, and his remains were buried at Detroit.

Dr. Duffield himself was a good soldier of Jesus Christ. He served so well and so long at first thought it seems strange, even unjust, that he should now be remembered principally as the author of a hymn. But, after all, such a hymn is the flower of a man's life, and holds the best he was and had. It is quite possible, too, that Dr. Duffield's hymn is the crown of his labors for Christ. He helped hundreds while he lived, but how many thousands have been encouraged and inspired by his brave song!

III

SUN OF MY SOUL, THOU SAVIOUR DEAR

THE TEXT OF THE HYMN

1   Sun of my soul, Thou Saviour Dear,
        It is not night if Thou be near;
    O may no earth-born cloud arise
        To hide Thee from Thy servant's eyes.

2   When the soft dews of kindly sleep
        My wearied eyelids gently steep,
    Be my last thought, how sweet to rest
        For ever on my Saviour's breast

3   Abide with me from morn till eve,
        For without Thee I cannot live;
    Abide with me when night is nigh,
        For without Thee I dare not die.

4   If some poor wandering child of Thine
        Have spurned to-day the voice Divine,
    Now, Lord, the gracious work begin;
        Let him no more lie down in sin.

5   Watch by the sick; enrich the poor
        With blessings from Thy boundless store;
    Be every mourner's sleep to-night,
        Like infants' slumbers, pure and light.

6   Come near and bless us when we wake,
          Ere through the world our way we take,
       Till in the ocean of Thy love
          We lose ourselves in heaven above.

Rev. John Keble, 1920

NOTE.–Six verses out of the fourteen of the original poem. The text is that of the second edition of *The Christian Year,* with (perhaps) a variation in the form of one word (see under "Some Points for Discussion.").

THE STORY OF THE HYMN

In June, 1827, a book of verse in two thin 16mo volumes was published at Oxford, England. It had the following title: "The Christian Year: Thoughts in Verse for the Sundays and Holydays throughout the Year." Beneath the title was the motto, "In quietness and in confidence shall be your strength." The author was a young clergyman, John Keble, but his name did not appear in the book. The secret of authorship was shared by a number of friends to whom he had submitted the manuscript, and gradually leaked out. For years he had been writing and revising his poems, and he wished to hold them back for still further polishing; perhaps not letting the book appear till after his death. But his aged father's urgent wish to see it in print impelled him to publish it without further delay.

The success of the book was immediate and extraordinary. Edition after edition was called for. In twenty-six years after publication forty-three editions, one hundred and eight thousand copies in all, were printed. Indeed, the sale of the book has gone on continuously up to the present time. The many who seemed most indifferent to its success, most unconscious of its merits, was the author himself. He never willingly talked about it or cared to hear it praised. That may be explained partly by his modesty and dissatisfaction with his work, but yet more from the fact that the book laid bare his inmost thoughts and feelings.

The Christian Year is not a continuous poem. It consists of a series of poems, one for each of the days and occasions for which services are provided in the Book of Common Prayer. These poems were not intended for singing, but for devotional reading as a poetical companion to the Prayer Book. And yet a good many hymns have been taken from them by compilers of hymn books.

The first service in the Prayer Book is the order for Morning Prayer. And the first poem in *The Christian Year* is called "Morning." Certain of its verses make one of our most familiar morning hymns, "New Every Morning is the Love" (*The Hymnal*, No. 6). The second service in the Prayer Book is the Order for Evening Prayer, and in *The Christian Year* the second poem is "Evening." It has fourteen verses, with the motto prefixed, "Abide with us, for it is towards evening, and the day is far spent." The third, seventh, twelfth, thirteenth, and fourteenth verses make up the familiar hymn, "Sun of My Soul," as printed in *The Hymnal* (No. 16) and here.

It would be interesting to know who it was with the wit to discover that so lovely and complete a hymn lay imbedded among the verses of a poem which, as a whole, is not a hymn at all. The great thing was to discern the precise point at which the hymn should begin. In a copy of the first edition of *The Christian Year* belonging to the present writer some one has mapped out a proposed hymn, beginning with the first verse of the poem, as follows: —

> "Tis gone, that bright and orbed blaze,
> Fast fading from our wistful gaze;
> Yon mantling cloud has hid from sight
> The last faint pulse of quivering light."

Such a hymn could not have won its way. As early as 1836 the accomplished Unitarian, John Hamilton Thom, made up for his *Selection* a hymn whose first verse was the ninth of the poem, beginning, "Thou Framer of the light and dark," followed by the last three verses as at present sung. A year earlier than that the Rev. Henry Venn Elliott (brother of the author of "Just as I Am") put into his *Psalms and Hymns* a selection of four verses, beginning with the "Sun of my soul" verse. His example was followed by other editors, some of them using additional verses. And, unless an earlier instance shall turn up, to him must be given the honor of discovering the hymn that lay imbedded in the poem. It is a curious fact that when Keble himself came to select the verses to be used in the *Salisbury Hymn Book*, 1857, he left out the "Sun of my soul" verse altogether, and began the hymn with "When the soft dews of kindly sleep." In this he has had few followers.

In England, as has been said, the success of *The Christian Year* was immediate. But England was more remote from the United States then than now, and the channels of fellowship between the Episcopal churches in the two countries were less open. Bishop Doane, of Burlington, New Jersey, had his attention called to the book in 1828, accidentally, by coming across a quotation from it. He edited and published in 1834, through Lea & Blanchard, Philadelphia, the first American edition of *The Christian Year*. His attempt, by means of notes, to make it serve also as a primer of, "the order, institutions, and services of the Church," together with his curious method of printing in italics all such lines throughout the book as especially pleased him, cause a smile of amusement to flit across the expression of one's appreciation of the Bishop's venture. It was not, however, until 1865 that "Sun of My Soul" was admitted among the hymns to be sung in Protestant Episcopal churches. The New England Unitarians (least in sympathy with Keble and yet most alert in seeing good in new things) were, as so often, the first to introduce the hymn into this country. In 1835 F.W.P Greenwood, pastor of King's Chapel, Boston, included it in his *Collection of Psalms and Hymns,* beginning the hymn with the first verse of the poem ("'Tis gone, that bright and orbed blaze"), and following that with the "Sun of my soul" verse and two more of those now so familiar. Several other Unitarian compilers followed Mr. Greenwood's lead. Henry Ward Beecher's *Plymouth Collection* of 1855 seems to have introduced the hymn into more orthodox circles; and in *The Sabbath Hymn Book* of the Andover professors, 1858, it appears, at length relieved of the incubus of a first verse that is not hymnic, as our familiar "Sun of My Soul, Thou Saviour Dear."

THE AUTHOR OF THE HYMN

John Keble was born at Fairford on April 25th, 1792. He was prepared for college by his father, a country clergyman (for whom the poet was named), and went up to Oxford "as a mere lad, home-bred and home-loving." Keble's home-training in a secluded parsonage, with the peaceful English landscape outside, and, within, the unquestioned reign of the old High Church prejudices, opinions, and piety, had a great part in making him what he was. It furnished the very atmosphere of the poetry of his after years.

While only eighteen he was graduated B.A., with double first-class honors, then counted a rare distinction. In those days, when scholarship outranked athletics, it made the shy, gentle lad "first man in Oxford." Cardinal Newman recalls that when he came there Keble's was the first name he heard, spoken of "with reverence rather than admiration," and confesses how abashed he felt in Keble's presence. This "reverence rather than admiration" seems to have been the common feeling toward Keble through all his life.

Keble was elected a Fellow of Oriel College, and remained in Oxford as a tutor and as examiner. He was ordained to the full ministry in 1816, and took a country curacy in addition to college duties. His mother's death, in 1823, brought him home to Fairford, and there, with the exception of a year as curate of Hursley, he stayed as his father's helper as long as the latter lived. It was while at Fairford that he published *The Christian Year.* Other than that, perhaps the most momentous thing he did in these years was preaching at Oxford in 1822 the famous Assize Sermon that, according to Newman, gave the start to the High Church or Oxford Movement, which transformed the Church of England. And of this movement Keble and Newman and Doctor Pusey were the leading spirits.

In 1835 Keble's father died. In that year he married and became Vicar of Hursley, a lovely village across the downs from Winchester. There he remained with entire contentment for the rest of his days, a famous man, but leading the life of a retired scholar and faithful country pastor. He rebuilt the village church, largely out of the profits of *The Christian Year;* and in his daily services and parish ministries carried out the church principles for which he stood.

Tender-hearted, kindly, gentle, and even playful in manner, Keble was none the less firm and decided in holding and advocating extreme High Church views. He gave himself very earnestly to forwarding "the movement," and had but scant regard for what he called "The Protestant party." But, unlike his friend Newman, he saw his way clear to remain in the Church of England. It is indeed impossible to think of him as making such a breach with his traditions and familiar surroundings, or as surviving it if made.

Keble's mind was that of a poet and not that of a logician. Intuition and feeling were more to him than reasoning, and he instinctively craved a comfortable support of authority as the sanction for opinions and acts. His character, in its childlikeness and purity, its entire unworldliness, its devotional fervor and spirit of consecration, was lovely indeed. Taken together with his power of substituting lofty poetry for polemics, it has given him extraordinary influence within the Church of England. Beyond its bounds that influence was necessarily limited by a theory of the church that withdrew him from any real sympathy and communion with his fellow Christians in other folds. His position in hymnody does not by any means correspond with the important place he occupies as a religious poet. The two lovely hymns extracted from the opening poems of *The Christian Year* come near to exhausting the materials that are available without an effort of piecing together unrelated passages. It is a book of meditative poetry and not of hymns. Keble's other poetical works include *Lyra Innocentium,* in which childhood is contemplated with the light from stained-glass windows falling upon it; and also a complete metrical version of the Psalms. The latter was never used as a hymn book, but is far superior to the average attempt to do a thing which, as Keble himself knew and acknowledged, is inherently impossible. The hymn beginning "God, the Lord, a King remaineth" (*The Hyman,* No. 89) is an example of Keble's renderings. From time to time he contributed a few other hymns to various books compiled by personal friends. He also assisted Earl Nelson in editing *The Salisbury*

Hymn Book of 1857. In this he printed his familiar wedding hymn, "The Voice that Breathed o'er Eden" (*The Hymnal,* No. 687).

Keble died on March 29ᵗʰ, 1866, at Bournemouth, where he had gone for the health of his wife, who survived him but six weeks. The last book he had in his hand was a hymn book – Roundell Palmer's *Book of Praise.* He had sent for it, because unable to recall all the verses of Bishop Ken's Evening Hymn, which he was accustomed to say in the night-watches by his wife. The graves of the poet and his wife are in Hursley church-yard.

IV

HOW FIRM A FOUNDATION, YE SAINTS OF THE LORD

THE TEXT OF THE HYMN

1   How firm a foundation, ye saints of the Lord,
         Is laid for your faith in His excellent word!
     What more can He say than to you He hath said, -
         You who unto Jesus for refuge have fled?
     To hide Thee from Thy servant's eyes.

2   "Fear not, I am with thee, O be not dismayed;
         I, I am thy god, and will still give thee aid;
     I'll strengthen thee, help thee, and cause thee to stand,
         Upheld by My righteous, omnipotent hand.

3   "When through the deep waters I call thee to go,
         The rivers of woe shall not thee overflow;
     For I will be with thee, thy troubles to bless,
         And sanctify to thee thy deepest distress.

4   "When through fiery trials thy pathway shall lie,
         My grace, all-sufficient, shall be thy supply;
     The flame shall not hurt thee; I only design
         The dross to consume, and thy gold to refine.

5   "E'en down to old age all My people shall prove
         My sovereign, eternal, unchangeable love;
     And when hoary hairs shall their temples adorn,
         Like lambs they shall still in My bosom be borne.

6   "The soul that on Jesus hath leaned for repose,
        I will not, I will not desert to his foes;
        That soul, though all hell should endeavor to shake,
        I'll never, no, never, no, never forsake."

"K____" in Rippon's "Selection of Hymns," 1787

NOTE.–Six verses out of seven: the text being taken from Dr. Rippon's book.

THE AUTHOR OF THE HYMN

Outside of the great hymn writers, few names are more familiar to a student of hymns than that of Dr. John Rippon. He was a pastor, from 1773 to 1836, of a Particular Baptist church in London. He had great reputation and influence both as man and as pastor; but of all the things he accomplished, the one best remembered is the hymn book he edited. He and his people were alike devoted to singing the psalms and hymns of Dr. Watts. Neither had any wish to supersede them, but Dr. Rippon had come to feel that hymns were needed on some subjects and occasions omitted by Dr. Watts. And hence he was led to publish, in the year 1787, a hymn book with this title: "A Selection of Hymns from the Best Authors, Intended to be an Appendix to Dr. Watts's Psalms and Hymns. By John Rippon, A.M."

It was a book of great merit, and was used widely and for long, many editions being printed in England and in this country; and Dr. Rippon is reputed to have accumulated a comfortable estate from his profits on the publication. The copy of the first edition in the possession of the present writer is graced by Dr. Rippon's portrait. But as this copy is in special binding, he ventures to hope that is one of a few prepared for personal friends, and that copies intended for use in worship were not so embellished. In any event Dr. Rippon must be credited with the very great services he rendered to hymnody. The remarkable feature of the book, which has given it permanent fame, is the great number of original hymns secured by him and there first printed. Many of these have been in use ever since.

From this copy of Dr. Rippon's book the photographer has reproduced for us, even to the light color of the ink, the page containing the most famous of these hymns. Looking upon the facsimile, we have before us the original text of "How Firm a Foundation," from the motto t the top to the editor's note at the bottom, with all the quaint capitalization, just as their eyes saw it who first found inspiration in singing it so long ago.

The facsimile gives us not only the text, but all that is actually known of the authorship of the hymn. Dr. Rippon's habit was to print the author's name above a hymn. This hymn is one of three to which the only signature is the letter "K" followed by a dash. The other two, beginning, "In songs of sublime adoration and praise," and "The Bible is justly esteemed," do not arouse much interest. But the authorship of this one seems to have been discussed from the first, and ever since has excited much curiosity and speculation. Such a problem has its own fascination. One cannot but think of the unknown writer, all unconscious that by signing his name to the hymn he would have won immortality, and of the other people who knew the secret, but are not here to answer our questions.

Naturally we turn to Dr. Rippon's preface, first of all, to see if it throws any light upon the matter. After speaking of the distinguished men who have contributed hymns, he adds: "In most Places, where the Names of the Authors were known, they are put at full Length, but the Hymns which are not so distinguished, or which have only a single Letter prefixed, were, many of them, composed by a Person unknown, or else have undergone some Considerable Alterations." What Dr. Rippon has in mind to say here is that many of the unsigned hymns were composed or recast by himself (the "Person unknown"), and that generally (but not always) he has given the author's name in full when he knew it. That is all, and it throws no light here.

As long Dr. Rippon lived to reprint his book, the signature to this hymn remained unchanged. After his death, and when the book has passed from the control of his representatives, an enlarged edition appeared, in which "K" is changed to "KIRKHAM." Who made the change, and for what reason, cannot now be known. Very likely it was based merely on hearsay. Certainly the new editor did not know who wrote the other two other hymns originally ascribed to "K", for they are left anonymous, even that letter being dropped. The ascriptions of authorship in this edition are so careless and full of errors as to carry little weight. In 1788 Thomas Kirkham published a collection of hymns, but those who have examined it say that this hymn is not among them. And there is no evidence that it was written by any one of the name of Kirkham.

Another solution of the puzzle was offered by Daniel Sedgwick. He was a second-hand bookseller of London, who collected hymn books and studied English hymns until he knew more of their history than any one else of his time. He suggested that "K" was probably put for Keith, meaning George Keith, a London bookseller, son-in-law of the famous Dr. Gill, and who was said to compose hymns based on his father-in-law's sermons. Dr. Julian, who examined Mr. Sedgwick's papers after his death, reports that his guess was based on nothing more substantial than a statement of an old woman whom Sedgwick met in an almshouse. But his name carried a certain authority, and his guess grew into a tradition. Many hymn books, even to the present time, ascribe the hymn to George Keith, sometimes with, and sometimes without, a mark of interrogation.

So the matter rested until taken up by a well-known editor of Boston, Mr. H.L. Hastings, who successfully solved the problem of the authorship of another hymn, "What a Friend We Have in Jesus." Mr. Hastings published the account of his investigations in his paper, *The Christian,* for May 1887, and it will be best to have the story in his own words:

"In preparing hymns and music for *Songs of Pilgrimage,* we were led to go over not only Dr. Rippon's hymn book but also his *Tune Book,* edited by Thomas Walker, who for a time led the singing in Dr. Rippon's church. We noticed that over the hymn in question was placed the name of a tune to which it was to be sung, which was Geard. On looking up that tune in the book, we found it was composed by R. Keene. There being but two tunes of that metre in the entire book, the thought arose, was the 'K' of the hymn the same person as the 'R. Keene,' to whose tune it was to be sung? Examining both hymn and tune, they seemed to be made for each other, and the evidence seemed to point to R. Keene as the author of the hymn; and we accordingly inserted it in *Songs of Pilgrimage*, with the original tune, and placed it under the name of R. Keene, with a query (?) to indicate uncertainty as to its origin.

"Visiting London, near the close of 1886, we called upon the venerable Charles Gordelier, and asked him, Who wrote 'How Firm a Foundation" He gave the names Kirkham, Keith, and Keene, but could give no definite reason for preferring one to another, until we laid the facts before him. Turning to Keene's tune, Geard, which he had copied into a book, he at once recognized it as the tune to which, fifty years before, they were accustomed to sing that hymn, and he also remembered that its author, R. Keene, was once a leader of the singing in Dr. Rippon's church, and that the hymn in question was said to have been written by a precentor in Dr. Rippon's church. After considerable thought, he recalled that half a century before, when he himself led the singing in the Baptist church, and used to meet with the different precentors from other meetings, he had heard the authorship of that hymn attributed to Keene, and he finally remembered that an aged woman named Edgehill, a member of Rippon's church, and the wife of a bookseller in Brick Lane, had told him that Keene was the author of that hymn.

"There might be various reasons why a musician and choir mater might put his name to a tune which he composed, while modesty, or other considerations, might cause him to append only his initial to a new hymn; and, in view of all the facts, we think we may consider the question settled, and definitely assign the authorship of the hymn to R. Keene, a precentor in Dr. Rippon's church, and the author to the tune Geard, to which it was sung."

Such was Mr. Hastings's conclusion, which for some reason has not attracted much attention; but it has had a striking confirmation at the hands of another investigator. In preparing a notice of this hymn for his

Dictionary of Hymnology, Dr. John Julian found that in Dr. Fletcher's Baptist *Collection* of 1822 the "K—"of Rippon was extended to "Kn" and in his edition of 1835, still further, to "Keen," while in the preface Dr. Fletcher stated that he was greatly assisted by Thomas Walker, and acknowledged his extensive acquaintance with sacred poetry. Now, this Thomas Walker was Dr. Rippon's precentor and the editor of his *Tune Book*, in which Geard appears. Taking this association into account, Dr. Julian argues that Dr. Walker based his ascription of authorship upon actual knowledge of the facts, and that "we are justified in concluding that the ascription to this hymn must be that of an unknown person of the name of Keen."

We have, then, a result practically the same from two independent investigations carried on in each case without knowledge of the other, and the reasonableness of such conclusion seems greatly strengthened by the coincidence. Mr. Hastings goes a step beyond Dr. Julian in fixing the identity of Keene. The present writer would add further particulars if he could. In the letters of the Rev. George Whitefield are many references to a Robert Keene, woolen draper in the Minories, London, who was Whitefield's faithful friend, a trustee of his Tabernacle, and who lived until 1793. But there seems to be nothing that would associate him with Dr. Rippon's Baptist hymn book.

THE STORY OF THE HYMN

The hymn seems to have come into immediate use upon its appearance in Dr. Rippon's book. Copies of the book were brought over into this country, and in 1790 this hymn was put into the hymn book of the Philadelphia Baptist Association. In 1792, only five years after its original publication, the whole book was reprinted in New York, so that the hymn began its career here almost as soon as in England, and for some reason it has won a more lasting popularity here than there. So familiar is the hymn to us, we imagine it to be ma standard wherever English hymns are sung. But such is not the fact. It never gained a foothold within the Church of England. It is not sung by the Wesleyans or Presbyterians of Great Britain, and but little by the Congregationalists. Dr. Horder, the best known hymnologist among the latter, speaks of it in his *Hymn Lover* as a hymn of no great merit. Its use, over there, is mostly among Baptists.

In this country, on the other hand, few hymns have been sung more generally or more enthusiastically. It has a part in the history of our common Christianity. Very likely the stirring tune to which it has for so long been sung in the United States is partly responsible for this popularity. That tune does not rightly belong to these words, and, as in the case of the hymn, its origin has never been certainly established. The statement of so many books that it was composed by John Reading rests on no real foundation. The familiar name, "Portuguese Hymn," is an error started by one who heard in the chapel of the Portuguese Embassy in London, and hastily assumed it to be a Portuguese melody. All that is actually known of the tune is that it was the music to a Latin Christmas hymn ("Adeste Fideles"), sung in Roman Catholic chapels throughout England as earlier as the middle of the eighteenth century. Our well-known "O Come, All Ye Faithful" (*The Hymnal*, No. 170), is a translation of the hymn to which the tune rightly belongs.

The position which the hymn "How Firm a Foundation," thus mated to the Christmas tune, has taken among us was strikingly illustrated in the late Spanish War. The incident is related in *The Sunday-School Times* for December 7th, 1901, by Lieutenant-Colonel Curtis Guild, Jr., late Inspector-General of the Seventh Army Corps. The corps was encamped along the hills at Quemados, near Havana, Cuba. On Christmas even of 1898 Colonel Guild sat before his tent in the balmy tropical night, chatting with a fellow-officer of Christmas and home. Suddenly from the camp of the Forty-ninth Iowa ran a sentinel's call, "Number ten: twelve o'clock, and all's well!"

"It was Christmas morning. Scarcely had the cry of the sentinel died away, when from the bandsmen's tents of that same regiment there rose the music of an old, familiar hymn, and one clear baritone led the chorus that quickly ran along those moonlit fields: 'How firm a foundation, ye saints of the Lord!' Another voice joined in, and another, and another, and in a moment the whole regiment was singing, and then the Sixth Missouri joined in, with the Fourth Virginia, and all the rest, till there, on the long ridges above the great city whence Spanish tyranny once went forth to enslave the New World, a whole American army corps was singing: —

> "'Fear not, I am with thee, O be not dismayed;
> I, I am thy God, and will still give thee aid;
> I'll strengthen thee, help thee, and cause thee to stand,
> Upheld by My righteous, omnipotent hand.'

"The Northern soldier knew the hymn as one he had learned beside his mother's knee. To the Southern soldier it was that and something more, it was the favorite hymn of General Robert E. Lee, and was sung at that great commander's funeral.

"Protestant and Catholic, South and North, singing together on Christmas day in the morning, — that's an American army!"

And if any one has felt a sense of impropriety in divorcing the old Christmas music from its proper words, surely he may feel that it came to its own again that morning. Such an incident, and what it implies, inclines one to rather the hope that "How Firm a Foundation" may never cease to be sung among us, and that it may never be set to any other tune.

V

LORD, WITH GLOWING HEART I'D PRAISE THEE

THE TEXT OF THE HYMN

1   Lord, with glowing heart I'd praise Thee
          For the bliss Thy love bestows,
    For the pardoning grace that saves me,
          And the peace that from it flows:
    Help, O God, my weak endeavor;
          This dull soul to rapture raise:
    Thou must light the flame, or never
          Can my love be warmed to praise.

2   Praise, my soul, the God that sought thee,
          Wretched wanderer, far astray;
    Found thee lost, and kindly brought thee
          From the paths of death away:
    Praise, with love's devoutest feeling,
          Him who saw thy guilt-born fear,
    And, the light of hope revealing
          Bade the blood-stained cross appear.

3   Lord, this bosom's ardent feeling
          Vainly would my lips express:
    Low before Thy footstool kneeling,
          Deign Thy suppliant's prayer to bless:
    Let Thy grace, my soul's chief treasure,
          Love's pure flame within me raise;
    And, since words can never measure,
          Let my life show forth Thy praise.

Francis Scott Key, 1817

NOTE.–The text is taken from Dr. Muhlenberg's *Church Poetry*, 1823.

THE STORY OF THE HYMN

To a patriotic American Christian it is a real satisfaction to find in the hymn book of his Church a hymn by the author of "The Star Spangled Banner." And the hymn is not unworthy of its place. A good judge, the Rev. Frederick M. Bird, in an essay upon the Hymnology of the Protestant Episcopal Church, called Mr. Key's hymn "as memorable a piece of work" as his "Star Spangled Banner." "It has," he says, "high devotional and fair literary merit, and is endeared to many thousands by long associations." There is, no doubt, a flavor of an older fashion in the rhetoric of the hymn, but its expression of Christian gratitude still rings true; and, as a matter of fact, the use of the hymn is more widespread to-day than ever before.

In 1823, the Rev. Dr. William A. Muhlenberg, afterward famous as the author of "I Would not Live Alway," printed a hymn book under the name of *Church Poetry*. "Here first (so far as is known) appeared Francis S. Key's very genuine hymn, 'Lord, with Glowing Praise I'd Praise Thee," says Mr. Bird in the essay already referred to. Such has been the general belief up to this time, and hence in every hymnal the hymn bears the date 1823. But in our present study we shall be able to make use of some facts not hitherto known.

In the autumn of 1900 the writer saw in a New York auction catalog the entry of a copy of this hymn in Mr. Key's autograph, which he secured. It is written on a half sheet of foolscap and inscribed in the margin, "Written by the author, F. Key, for Sylvester Nash." Hitherto only three eight-line verses of the hymn had been known to hymnologists, as printed in Dr. Muhlenberg's book and always since. But the autograph copy has an additional verse (or two of four lines each) as reproduced in the accompanying facsimile. This was the original third verse, preceding the last one as here printed.

And now, as regards the date. In December of 1901, while having some part in the rearrangement of the library of the Presbyterian

Historical Society in Philadelphia, the writer took the opportunity of examining some old periodicals, on the chance of what he might find. Among them were three volumes of *The Christian Messenger*, an insectaria religious magazine, edited and published by Joshua T. Russell, in Baltimore. At page 288 of the first volume, at the end of the number for Saturday, September 6th, 1817, he found the original printing of this hymn. It is printed in eight four-line verses, and is prefaced by this note: —

> "The following Hymn was composed by a gentleman, formerly a resident of this city, distinguished for his eminent talents and exemplary piety."

This little discovery changes the accepted date of the hymn from 1823 to 1817. The additional eight lines of the manuscript are included in the hymn in the magazine, and this seems to be the first and last time they have been printed until now. Dr. Muhlenberg chose to omit them from his hymn book in 1823. And since then every one else, even the editor of Mr. Key's poems (which were gathered up and published in 1857), seems completely to have lost sight of them.

In 1826 Mr. Key's hymn, in its three-verse form, was given a place in the *Hymns of the Protestant Episcopal Church,* and it has retained that place in the hymnals from time to time authorized for use in that Church. It was introduced to a much wider company when, in 1930, the Rev. Joshua Leavitt included it in his very popular collection, *The Christian Lyre.* This was the book the light and secular character of whose music caused such grief to the heart of Thomas Hastings. Designed for revival and social meetings, it found its way into the more formal services of many Presbyterian churches, as a welcome substitute for the authorized psalmody. It cannot be said, however, that by this means, or any other, Mr. Key's hymn became generally familiar to Presbyterians until a much later date. *The Presbyterian Hymnal* of 1874 was the first authorized book to contain it. A peculiar feature in the long career of this hymn is that so little music should have been composed for it. Even now the words can hardly be said to be associated with any particular tune.

THE AUTHOR OF THE HYMN

Over the grave of Francis Scott Key, at Frederick, Maryland, there was placed in 1989 an impressive monument. His figure in bronze stands on a granite base. He is represented at the moment of discovery that "our flag was still there," his right arm extended toward it, and the left waving aloft his hat in an exultant salute. It is a striking representation of the way in which Mr. Key himself stands before the minds of his countrymen. They think of him always as in that attitude. To them he is always the man who wrote "The Star Spangled Banner." The one hour outshines the life so much in men's eyes that the life has become obscure.

It is none the less pleasant to know how worthy that life was before and after its great event; to find the home life as attractive as the patriotism, to find the grace of the gentleman and the earnestness of the Christian at one with the gifts of the poet.

No extended life of Mr. Key has been published, but it seems as if (like that editor who put the note before his hymn) every one who wrote of him felt called upon to praise him.

Mr. Key was the son of John Ross Key, a man of means and high social position, and a self-sacrificing patriot of the Revolution; and was born on his father's estate, Terra Rubra, Frederick, Maryland, on August 1st, 1779. He was educated at St. John's College, Annapolis, and in 1802 married the representative of another distinguished Maryland family, Mary Tayloe-Lloyd, whose ancestral home, with its wainscoted drawing-room, has stood in Annapolis from 1709 until now.

Mr. Key practiced law in Frederick for some years, afterward moving to Georgetown, D.C. For three terms he was district attorney of the District of Columbia. As a lawyer he seems not to have been to severe studies, but yet competent, with a ready mind full of resources and equal to the occasion. He had, too, more than a little of the gifts of the orator; was natural and earnest, and easily kindled into passion. In person he was slight, and of extraordinary vigor both in mind and body; walking, when an elderly man, with the light and elastic gait of a boy, and highly charged with electricity through his whole system. He was absolutely fearless, ardent, impulsive, frank, outspoken; not without the defects of his qualities. Not always recognized by passing acquaintances as being all that he was, and yet always as being a gentleman. He was cheerful, and liked social life and hospitalities, and excelled in bright conversation. Of real warmth of heart, he loved his friends with great loyalty and his family with tender devotion.

Mr. Key was a member of the Protestant Episcopal Church, of the type known as Evangelical. He loved his own Church, but one who had been his rector (Rev. John T. Brooke) has taken pains to record in a Memorial Discourse that he "had no sympathy whatever with the later attempts of *individuals,* at different periods, to erect high and exclusive fences upon the original peculiarities of the church." He was in sympathy with good men of every name, and ready to worship and cooperate with them. Though burdened with the care of a very large family and heavy professional duties, he was habitually bus in Christian work to a degree that excited the wonder of his pastor. Ready to officiate as a lay-reader when needed, a fervent participant in social meetings for prayer, "he found much time to visit the sick, to comfort the mourning, to confer with the enquiring, to warn the careless; and he stood ever ready, at a moment's warning, to lift his voice in behalf of any of the great public charities of the day."

Mr. Key and his wife were both slave-holders by inheritance, but deplored the existence of the institution of slavery. Mr. Key gave much thought to his own negroes, and regularly held Sunday-school for them; in his neighborhood he was proverbially the colored man's friend, their unpaid advocate in the courts, their helper in time of trouble. He was among the first to think out the scheme of African colonization as the most hopeful remedy for a complicated situation. In connection with his friend Bishop Meade, he traveled much and worked hard to promote the cause, to which he became ardently devoted. His income was always carefully apportioned to provide a fund for his charities, and among his last words were his directions where to find and how to employ the moneys then on hand for such uses.

"Good men are great blessings to the community" – it was so that Mr. Key's pastor began the Memorial Discourse. "But they must die" — so it continued. And though a commonplace, one can understand how hard it must have been to apply the phrase to one so very much alive as he. Mr. Key died in Baltimore, January 11th, 1843. In addition to the monument over his grave erected by popular subscription, a statue of him also stands in Golden Gate Park, San Francisco, provided by the will of James Lick, the California millionaire.

But his song is his monument. Toward the end of the War of 1812 he learned that a friend and neighbor had been taken from his home by the British forces and was held as a prisoner on board the admiral's ship. He at once determined to intercede for his friend's release, and secured from the government such papers as were necessary to his purpose. Visiting the squadron of the British on the Potomac under a flag of truce, that summer day in 1814, he was detained under guard, for an attack on Baltimore was just about to begin. Anxiously he paced the deck through the long night of the bombardment, until he caught the dawn's early light on the flag still waving over Fort McHenry. The attack had failed. He was released with the song in his heart, and most of it roughly drafted on the back of a letter before he reached the shore. The next day it was printed on handbills, and men were singing it, as they have been ever since.

VI

MY FAITH LOOKS UP TO THEE

THE TEXT OF THE HYMN

1   My faith looks up to Thee,
Thou Lamb of Calvary,
    Saviour Divine:
No hear me while I pray,
Take all my guilt away,
O let me from this day
    Be wholly Thine.

2   May Thy rich grace impart
Strength to my fainting heart,
    My zeal inspire;
As Thou hast died for me,
O may my love to Thee
Pure, warm, and changeless be,
    A living fire.

3   While life's dark maze I tread,
And griefs around me spread,
    Be Thou my Guide;
Bid darkness turn to day,
Wipe sorrow's tears away,
Nor let me ever stray
    From Thee aside.

4   When ends life's transient dream,
        When death's cold, sullen stream
          Shall o'er me roll,
        Blest Saviour, then, in love,
        Fear and distrust remove;
        O bear me safe above,
          A ransomed soul.

Ray Palmer, 1830

NOTE.–The text is taken from his *Hymns and Sacred Pieces,* 1865. As regards a different reading in the original printing of the hymn, see under "Some Points for Discussion." (3).

THE STORY OF THE HYMN

"Look in thy heart, and write," said the muse to Sir Philip Sidney; and no language could reveal more clearly the source of this hymn. Its words "were born of my own soul," the author said long afterward to Dr. Cuyler. It becomes at once evident, therefore, that we must be altogether dependent upon such disclosures as the author chose to make for any real knowledge of the origin of the hymn. Happily for us the publication of inaccurate and apocryphal accounts of the matter (already alluded to in the preface of this book), together with a wish to escape from "the necessity of replying to letters of inquiry which have been received in inconvenient numbers," led Dr. Palmer (in an appendix to his *Poetical Works,* 1876) to narrate the circumstances and experience out of which the hymn arose:

"Immediately after graduating at Yale College, in September, 1830, the writer went to the city of New York, by previous engagement, to spend a year in teaching for two or three hours each day in a select school for young ladies. This private institution, which was patronized by the best class of families, was under the "direction of an excellent Christian lady connected with St. George's Church, the rector of which was then the good Dr. James Milnor. It was in Fulton Street, west of Broadway, and a little below Church Street on the south side of the way. That whole section of the city, now covered with immense stores and crowded with business, was then occupied by genteel residences. The writer resided in the family on the lady who kept the school, and it was there that the hymn was written.

"It had no *external* occasion whatever. Having been accustomed almost from childhood, through an inherited propensity perhaps, to the occasional expression of what his heart felt in the form of verse, it was in accordance with this habit, and in an hour when Christ, in the riches of His grace and love, was so vividly apprehended as to fill the soul with deep emotion, that the piece was composed. There was not the slightest thought of writing for another eye, least of all writing a hymn for Christian worship. Away from outward excitement, in the quiet of his chamber, and with a deep consciousness of his own needs, the writer transferred as faithfully as he could to paper what at the time was passing within him. Six stanzas were composed, and imperfectly written, first on a loose sheet, and then accurately copied into a small morocco-covered book, which for such purposes the author was accustomed to carry in his pocket. This first complete copy is still – 1875 – preserved. It is well remembered that when writing the last line, 'A ransomed soul,' the thought that the whole work of redemption and salvation was involved in those words, and suggested the theme of eternal praises, moved the writer to a degree of emotion that brought abundant tears.

"A year or two after the hymn was written, and when no one, so far as can be recollected, had ever seen it, Dr. Lowell Mason met the author in the street in Boston, and requested him to furnish some hymns for a Hymn and Tune Book which, in connection with Dr. Hastings of New York, he was about to publish. The little book containing it was shown him, and he asked a copy. We stepped into a store together, and a copy was made and given him, which without much notice he put in his pocket. On sitting down at home and looking it over, he became so much interested in it that he wrote for it the tune 'Olivet,' in which it has almost universally been sung. Two or three days afterward we met again in the street, when, scarcely waiting to salute the writer, he earnestly exclaimed, 'Mr. Palmer, you may live many years and do many good things, but I think you will be best known to posterity as the author of 'My Faith Looks Up to Thee.'"

The hymn and tune book referred to by Dr. Palmer, in which the hymn first appeared, came out in twelve parts in 1831-32, and was called *Spiritual Songs for Social Worship*. Numerous editions of the book were printed; before long the hymn and its tune became widely sung and began to be copied into other books. In 1842 it was introduced into England through the Rev. Andrew Reed's *Hymn Book*. The hymn is to-day among those most familiar in evangelical churches of both countries. The statement often made that it now appears in every hymn book is, of course, not true. That is not true of any hymn. But it is well known and as well loved as any American hymn. It seems to many people like a part of their own spiritual life.

THE AUTHOR OF THE HYMN

Ray Palmer was the son of the Hon. Thomas Palmer of Little Compton, Rhode Island, and was born at that place on November 12th, 1808. In his thirteenth year he became clerk in a dry-goods store at Boston, and while there he connected himself with the Park Street Church. His thoughts turned toward the ministry, and he spent three years preparing for college at Phillips Academy, Andover, and in 1830 was graduated from Yale. Then came the years of teaching and of preparation for the ministry, first at New York and afterward at New Haven. He was ordained in 1835, becoming pastor of the Central Congregational Church of Bath, Maine, where he remained until 1850. From then until 1866 he was pastor of the First Congregational Church of Albany, New York. In 1866 he became the Corresponding Secretary of the American Congregational Union, removing to New York City, and holding that laborious post until 1878. He resigned his secretaryship in that year and had already removed to Newark, New Jersey.

The real occasion of this resignation was the failure of Dr. Palmer's health. He suffered from a nervous affection causing an uncertainty, at times even a stagger, in his walk. But for some years after giving up his work in New York he continued in active service in connection with the Belleville Avenue Congregational Church, of Newark. By a unique arrangement Dr. Palmer became its "pastor," having especial charge of visiting the people; while Dr. George H. Hepworth was its "preacher," and Dr. Williams Hayes Wards its "superintendent of mission work." At Newark, in 1882, Dr. Palmer gathered about him a distinguished and affectionate company to celebrate the golden anniversary of his wedding to Miss Ann M. Ward, of New York. But the warning of his approaching end soon followed. He died at Newark on March 29th, 1887.

Dr. Palmer was the author of a number of books. His prose writings were generally that of a devotional character, but included *Hints on the Formation of Religious Opinions* (1860), of which several editions were printed. His hymns and other verse appeared in successive volumes: *Hymns and Sacred Pieces* (1865), *Hymns of My Holy Hours* (1868), *Home, or the Unlost Paradise* (1868), *Complete Poetical Works* (1876), and *Voices of Hope and Gladness* (1881). Dr. Palmer's poetical work was voluminous enough to fill an 8vo volume of more than three hundred and fifty pages. It is always pure and often graceful, and written in easily flowing verse, but the body of his miscellaneous poetry does not attain such elevation of thought or distinction of form as would recommend it to the student of literature.

In estimating his poetry it is only fair to remember that Dr. Palmer's life "for more than forty years was unremittingly devoted to the absorbing duties of a Christian minister, and for more than three-fourths of this period to the manifold labors of a city Pastor. Poetry, instead of filling any prominent places in the programme of his life, had been only the occupation of the few occasional moments that could be redeemed from severer, and generally very prosaic, forms of work."

When we turn from the miscellaneous poetry to the hymns, we have a different situation and a happier result. There was nothing in Dr. Palmer's circumstances to interfere with the production of hymns. They were quite in line with his thought and work. And the hymn-form furnished precisely the medium through which his purely devotional spirit and gift for graceful verse could find their most spontaneous express. It is among the hymn writers that Dr. Palmer finds his proper place, and by many he is considered to be the foremost hymn writer in America. He is distinguished not only for the excellence of his best hymns, but for the number of his hymns that are in all ways good. And to them must he added his translations of Latin hymns, in which he was especially successful. Several of his hymns are favorites; and yet what Lowell Mason prophesied has come to pass, and Dr. Palmer is best known as the author of "My Faith Looks Up to Thee."

Dr. Palmer's character corresponded to his hymns. One who knew him well has recently spoken of him to the present writer as "One of the loveliest of men. He was exceedingly agreeable in conversation, which always had a spiritual tone," the same friend went on to say. "There was a certain saintliness in his manner and personality. He was gentle in his ways of speech, but had very deep feelings, which often came to the surface in conversation. His religious character was never better illustrated than when he was drawn out to speak of his famous hymn: the usual egotism of an author was so overcome by a feeling of simple gratitude for what the hymn had accomplished."

Dr. Palmer's portrait illustrates the description of his personal appearance given by his friend Dr. Theodore Cuyler (in *Recollections of a Long Life)*: "He was short in stature, but his erect form and habit of brushing his hair high over his forehead gave him a commanding look. He was the impersonation of genuine enthusiasm."

VII

LEAD, KINDLY LIGHT,
AMID THE ENCIRCLING GLOOM

THE TEXT OF THE HYMN

1 Lead, kindly Light, amid the encircling gloom,
    Lead Thou me on;
  The night is dark, and I am far from home;
    Lead Thou me on:
  Keep Thou my feet; I do not ask to see
  The distant scene,— one step enough for me.

2 I was not ever thus, nor prayed that Thou
    Shouldst lead me on;
  I loved to choose and see my path; but now
    Lead Thou me on.
  I loved the garish day, and, spite of fears,
  Pride ruled my will: remember not past years.

3 So long Thy power hath blest me, sure it still
    Will lead me on
  O'er moor and fen, o'er crag and torrent, till
    The night is gone;
  And with the morn those angel faces smile,
  Which I have loved long since, and lost awhile.

    Rev. (afterward Cardinal) John Henry Newman, 1833

NOTE.–The text is taken from Newman's *Verses on Various Occasions,*
1867; and agrees with that in *Lyra Apostolica.*

THE STORY OF THE HYMN

This much-loved hymn is always spoken of as having been written by Cardinal Newman, and the fact that Protestants love to sing it is used to show the real unity of Christians, whether Roman Catholic or Protestant. But as a matter of fact the hymn was not written by Cardinal Newman, nor even by a Roman Catholic. It was written by the Rev. John Henry Newman, a young clergyman of the Church of England, twelve years before he went into the Church of Rome; and at a time when, as he himself tells us, he had no thought of leaving the Church of England. Indeed, Cardinal Newman said in 1882 to Lord Ronald Gower (who reports it in his *Old Diaries*) that the hymn did not represent his feeing at that time. "For we Catholics" he said, with a quiet smile, "believe we have found the light."

The hymn is so much a part of its author's life that the story of his hymn and his life must be told together. The son of John Newman, a London banker, he was born, on February 21st, 1801, within sound of Bow Bells. He was an imaginative boy, and so superstitious that he used constantly to cross himself on going into the dark. He never could explain what started him into such a practice, for his surrounding were those of Evangelical Protestantism, and his own beliefs were Calvinistic, including the opinion that the Pope was anti-Christ. At his conversion, when fifteen years old, his mind became filled with that sense of communion with God which possessed him all his life, and made outwards things seem as nothing to him. A curious imagination took hold of him at the same time that it was God's will that he should live a single life. This feeling never left him.

Newman went up to Oxford, and was graduated from Trinity College in 1820; remaining there first as a fellow, and then as a tutor, of Oriel. In 1824 he was ordained, and in 1828 was appointed vicar of St. Mary's Church, at Oxford. Then he began to preach those sermons which had so extraordinary an influence, and are though by many the greatest of the century. Meantime his religious opinions were gradually changing under those High Church influences at Oxford which had their beginnings in Keble's *Christian Year*. Especially marked was the influence of his friend and fellow tutor, Hurrell Froude. Froude changed Newman's hostility to the Church of Rome to deep admiration, and taught him to look upon the Reformation as a mistake. "He fixed deep in me," says Newman, "the idea that devotion to the Blessed Virgin, and he led me gradually to believe in the Real Presence."

To this period of change and unrest the hymn belongs. The anxieties that lay behind it and the circumstances out of which it sprang are fully narrated in Newman's *Apologia pro Vita Suo;* and certainly no one would care to learn of them from any other source:

"While I was engaged in writing my work upon the Arians great events were happening at home, which brought out into form and passionate expression the various beliefs which had so gradually been winning their way into my mind ... The great Reform agitation was going on around me as I wrote. The Whigs had come into power; Lord Grey had told the Bishops to set their house in order, and some of the Prelates had been insulted and threatened in the streets of London. The vital question was, how were we to keep the Church from being liberalized? There was such an apathy on the subject in some quarters, such imbecile alarm in others; the true principles of Churchmanship seemed so radically decayed, and there was such distraction in the councils of the Clergy... With the Establishment thus divided and threatened, thus ignorant of its true strength, I compared that fresh vigorous Power of which I was reading in the first centuries... I said to myself, 'Look on this picture and on that'; I felt dismay at her prospects, anger and scorn at her do-nothing perplexity. I thought that if Liberalism once got a footing within her, it was sure of the victory in the event. I saw that Reformation principles were powerless to rescue her. As to leaving her, the thought never crossed my imagination; still I ever kept her before me that there was something greater than the Established Church, and that was the Church Catholic and Apostolic, set up from the beginning, of which she was but the local presence and the organ. She was nothing unless she was this. She must be dealt with strongly or she would be lost. There was need of a second reformation.

"At this time, I was disengaged from college duties, and my health had suffered from the labor involved in the composition of my Volume

... I was easily persuaded to join Hurrell Froude and his Father, who were going to the south of Europe for the health of the former.

"We set out in December, 1832 ... I went to various coasts of the Mediterranean; parted with my friends at Rome; went down for the second time to Sicily without companion, at the end of April; ... the strangeness of foreign life threw me back into myself... England was in my thoughts solely, and the news from England came rarely and imperfectly. The bill for the Suppression of Irish Sees was in progress, and filled my mind ... It was the success of the Liberal cause which fretted me inwardly...

"Especially when I was left by myself, the thought came upon me that deliverance is wrought not by the many but by the few, not body bodies but by persons ... I began to think that I had a mission... When we took leave of Monsignore Wiseman, he had courteously expressed a wish that we might make a second visit to Rome; I said with great gravity, 'We have a work to do in England.' I went down at once to Sicily, and the presentiment grew stronger. I struck into the middle of the island, and fell ill of a fever in Leonforte. My servant thought I was dying, and begged me for my last directions. I gave them, as he wished; but I said, 'I shall not die.' I repeated, 'I shall not die, for I have not sinned against light.' I have never been able quite to make out what I meant.

"I got to Castro-Giovanni, and was laid up there for nearly three weeks. Towards the end of May I left for Palermo, taking three days for the journey. Before starting from my inn in the morning of May 26th or 27th, I sat down on my bed and began to sob violently. My servant, who had acted as my nurse, asked what ailed me. I could only answer him, 'I have a work to do in England.'

"I was aching to get home; yet for want of a vessel was kept at Palermo for three weeks. I began to visit the Churches, and they calmed my impatience, though I did not attend any services ... At last I got off in an orange boat, bound for Marseilles. Then it was that I wrote the lines, 'Lead, kindly light,' which have since become well known. We were becalmed a whole week in the Straits of Bonifacio. I was writing verses the whole time of my passage. At length I got to Marseilles, and set off for England."

We can now understand the hymn. We can see into the shadows that encircled him who wrote it, — the sickness and depression, the loneliness, the dark thoughts of the Church he still clung to. We know his sense of being called by God to do a work at home without seeing what its end might be. We hear his answer to the call in his renunciation of all pride of leadership into God's hands, his cry for only light enough to see one step ahead, his confidence that God will find his path. "For years," Newman said in another connection, "I must have had something of a habitual notion, though it was latent, and had never led me to distrust my own convictions, that my mind had not found its ultimate rest, and that in some sense or other I was on a journey. During the same passage across the Mediterranean in which I wrote 'Lead kindly light,' I also wrote the verses which are found in the *Lyra* under the head of 'Providences,' beginning 'When I look back.' This was in 1833; and, since I have begun this narrative, I have found a memorandum under the date of September 7th, 1829, in which I speak of myself as 'now in my rooms in Oriel College, slowly advancing, &c., and led on by God's hand blindly, not knowing whither He is taking me.'"

The date of the hymn is June 16th, 1833. On the Sunday following Newman's return from his southern trip it happened that Mr. Keble preached at Oxford his famous sermon on "The National Apostasy." "I have ever considered and kept the day," Newman says, "as the start of the religious movement of 1833."

Newman returned in time to become the centre of that very powerful movement to undo the work of the Reformation in England. But he grew so much out of sympathy with all that Protestantism stands for, that, in 1845, he asked to be received into the Roman Catholic Church. His secession was a great blow to many of his friends, to none more than Keble, to whom it was a life-long sorrow. It caused also intense excitement and bitterness of feeling, the famous *Apologia* having been written in answer to charges of insincerity made by Charles Kingsley.

Newman continued a devout Roman Catholic, and in 1879 was made a cardinal by the Pope, dying in 1890. It was a strange career of a wonderfully gifted man. But no one doubts his sincerity or the depth and purity of his religion.

Newman's verses were first printed in *The British Magazine* for March, 1834, and then in 1836 in the *Lyra Apostolica*, a little book in which the contributions to the Magazine of Newman, Keble, and other kindred spirits, were gathered up. In 1846 the verses were included by Longfellow and Johnson in their *Book of Hymns*. Unfortunately they had found them in a newspaper as beginning "Send kindly light," and so they printed them. In 1865 Dr. Charles S. Robinson printed them with the same opening in his *Songs for the Sanctuary*. He explained (in *The Congregationalist,* 1890) that the change was made by a "literary friend" who first brought the hymn to his notice, and who assumed that the form "Lead, kindly Light" was a typographical error, arising from the close resemblance of the words *Lead* and *Send* in careless manuscript. It is surely an instance of loyalty to friendship that Dr. Robinson persisted in so misprinting the hymn in all editions of that popular book up to the day of his death. And so the hymn stands in the more recent issues by the Century Company, now owning the plates of the book. The present familiarity and popularity of the hymn began with its inclusion in 1868 in the *Appendix to Hymns Ancient and Modern*. Cardinal Newman's connection with hymnody by no means ends with this hymn. From his long poem, "The Dream of Gerontius," has been taken the fine hymn beginning, "Praise to the Holiest in the height" (*The Hymnal,* No. 429). He also published two collections of Latin hymns taken from the Breviaries, and made numerous and excellent translations from them.

VIII

MY COUNTRY, 'TIS OF THEE

THE TEXT OF THE HYMN

1   My country, 'tis of thee,
     Sweet land of liberty,
         Of thee I sing;
     Land where my fathers died,
     Land of the pilgrims' pride,
     From every mountain side
         Let freedom ring.

2   My native country, thee,
     Land of the noble free,
         Thy name I love;
     I love thy rocks and rills,
     Thy woods and templed hills;
     My heart with rapture thrills
         Like that above.

3   Let music swell the breeze,
     And ring from all the trees
         Sweet freedom's song:
     Let mortal tongues awake;
     Let all that breathe partake;
     Let rocks their silence break,
         The sound prolong.

4   Our father's God, to Thee,
       Author of liberty,
         To Thee we sing:
       Long may our land be bright
       With freedom's holy light;
       Protect us by Thy night,
         Great God, our King

Rev. Samuel Francis Smith, 1832

NOTE.–This is the text of the hymn as originally written, and which Dr. Smith expressed himself as feeling unauthorized to alter in any particular.

THE STORY OF THE HYMN

At a reunion of the famous Class of 1829, of Harvard College, one of its members referred to a classmate in this way:—

"And there's a nice youngster of excellent pith,—
Fate tried to conceal him by naming him Smith;
But he shouted a song for the brave and the free,—
Just read on his medal, 'My country,' 'of thee!'"

It was Dr. Oliver Wendell Holmes who read the poem, and it was his friend and classmate, Samuel Francis Smith, who wrote "My Country, 'tis of Thee."

He was a Boston boy, born under the sound of the Old North Church chimes on October 21st, 1808. After being graduated at Harvard he began to study for the ministry; and it was while at Andover Theological Seminary, in February, 18322, that he wrote the hymn.

In 1831 or thereabouts Mr. William C. Woodbridge, a distinguished educator, had visited Germany for the purpose of studying the system of German common schools. Among their peculiarities he noted that much attention was given to children's music, and he brought home with him a large number of music books, especially such as were used in the German schools. In Boston just then Mr. Lowell Mason was interesting himself in the music of the churches, and was engaged in training the Sunday-school children to sing, with a few of fitting them to take their places in the choirs. There was quite a scarcity of songs and tunes suitable for children's use, and Mr. Woodbridge placed the entire collection which he had brought from Germany into Mr. Mason's hands. But in all these books the music was set to German words, and of that language Mr. Mason had no knowledge.

And this fact was the occasion which led to the writing of the hymn "America." Dr. Smith during his lifetime furnished many accounts of the circumstances, which, of course, he alone knew. While all of these accounts are in substantial agreement, much the best of them was that written for *The Outlook*, and printed in the number for November 23rd, 1895:

"At that time," says Dr. Smith, "I was a student in the Theological Seminary at Andover. One day [Mr. Mason] bought me the whole mass of his books, some bound and some in pamphlet form, and said, in his simple childlike way, 'There, Mr. Woodbridge has brought me these books. I don't know what is in them. I can't read German, but you can. I wish you would look over them as you find time, and if you fall in with anything I can use, any hymns or songs for the children, I wish you would translate them into English poetry; or, if you prefer, compose hymns or songs of your own of the same metre and accent with the German, so that I can use them.'

"I accepted the trust not unwillingly, as an agreeable recreation from graver studies, and from time to time gave him the results of my efforts. Thus he was furnished with several hymns for the *Spiritual Songs*, which he was issuing in numbers; also for the *Juvenile Lyre*, the first book of children's music ever published in this country, in which most of the songs were my own translations from Naegeli and other German composers.

"One dismal day in February, 1832, about half an hour before sunset, I was turning over the leaves of one of the music books, when my eye rested on the tune which is now known as 'America.' I liked the spirited movement of it, not knowing it, at that time, to be 'God Save the King." I glanced at the German words and saw that they were patriotic, and instantly felt the impulse to write a patriotic hymn of my own, adapted to the tune. Picking up a scrap of waste paper which lay near me, I wrote at once, probably within half an hour, the hymn 'America,' as it is now known everywhere. The whole hymn stands to-day as it stood on the bit of waste paper, five or six inches long and two and a half wide."

Mr. Smith had no suspicion that he had in that short half hour made his name imperishable. He gave the song soon afterward to Mr. Mason, with some others, and thought no more about it. On the Fourth of July of that same year Mr. Mason brought it out at a children's celebration in the Park Street Church, Boston. From there it soon found its way into the public schools of that city, and then of other paces, and into picnics and patriotic celebrations everywhere, and finally into the hymn books of the various denominations. The whole history of the hymn and its present position are summed up in a remark once made by the author himself: "The people took it into their hearts." To-day it is called the national hymn, but it is not made so by any formal decree of adoption. It is the national hymn simply because the people that compose the nation love it, and on any occasion when their hearts are fired by patriotic feelings, use this hymn spontaneously to express those feelings.

THE AUTHOR OF THE HYMN

Samuel F. Smith was graduated from Andover Seminary the same y ear in which he wrote the hymn. For a year and a half after gradua-tion, he was the editor of the *Baptist Missionary Magazine*. In February, 1834, he was ordained and became pastor of the Baptist Church in Waterville, Maine. He continued as pastor there for eight years, serving also as Professor of Modern Languages in Waterville College, now Colby University: for among Dr. Smith's other gifts was that of acquiring languages. During his life he became familiar with no less than fifteen, and a visitor to him in his eighty-sixth year found him on the lookout for a suitable text-book with which he might begin the study of the Russian language.

In 1842 Dr. Smith became pastor of the First Baptist Church of Newton, Massachusetts, when he removed to Newton Centre. There for more than half a century he lived in a simple way with his family in the wide, brown frame dwelling of two stories, which has been the goal of so many sight-seers. He was pastor there for twelve years and a half, and then Secretary of the Missionary Union for fifteen, spending two of them abroad visiting missionary stations.

Dr. Smith led a very busy, active life, preaching, editing, writing, studying. For 1842 to 1848 he was editor of *The Christian Review.* He was one of the editors of *The Psalmist* (1843), a most successful Baptist hymn book, and compiled several collections of verse, of which *Rock of Ages* is the best known. He was also the author of *The Life of Joseph Grafton* (1848), *Missionary Sketches* (1879), *The History of Newton, Massachusetts,* (1884), and of *Missionary Sketches* (1884), which embodied a later tour among foreign fields.

His verse writing was a recreation rather than an occupation, and he made no claim to be counted among the poets. Certainly the large volume of his verse gathered at the close of his life under the editor-ship of his friend General Carrington would yield no sure support for such a claim. He wrote, however, many successful hymns, of which "The Morning Light is Breaking," (*The Hymnal*, No. 386), is especially familiar. But, no matter what he accomplished or where he went, it was always as the author of "My Country, 'tis of Thee" that he was recognized and welcomed, and was honored as such at a public celebra-tion in Music Hall, Boston, during the last year of his life. Dr. Smith lived to be eighty-seven y ears old, active and busy until the evening of Saturday, Nov. 16th, 1895. On that evening he took the train for Readville, near Boston, where he was to preach the next day. Just as he entered the car, turning to speak with a friend, he gasped for breath, threw his hands in the air, and fell backward in death.

IX

ONWARD, CHRISTIAN SOLDIERS

THE TEXT OF THE HYMN

1   Onward, Christian soldiers,
        Marching as to war,
    With the cross of Jesus
        Going on before:
    Christ the Royal Master
        Leads against the foe;
    Forward into battle,
        See, His banners go.
                Onward, Christian soldiers,
                    Marching as to war,
                With the cross of Jesus
                    Going on before.

2   At the sign of triumph
        Satan's host doth flee;
    On then, Christian soldiers,
        On to victor:
    Hell's foundation quiver
        At the shout of praise;
    Brothers, lift your voices,
        Loud your anthems raise.
                Onward, etc.

3   Like a mighty army
          Moves the Church of God;
      Brothers, we are treading
          Where the saints have trod;
      We are not divided,
          All one body we,
      One in hope and doctrine,
          One in charity.
              Onward, etc.

4   Crowns and thrones may perish,
          Kingdoms rise and wane,
      But the Church of Jesus
          Constant will remain;
      Gates of hell can never
          'Gainst that Church prevail;
      We have Christ's own promise,
          And that cannot fail.
              Onward, etc.

5   Onward, then, ye people,
          Join our happy throng,
      Blend with ours your voices
          In the triumph-song;
      Glory, laud, and honor
          Unto Christ the King;
      This through countless ages
          Men and angels sing.
              Onward, etc.

Rev. Sabine Baring-Gould, 1865

NOTE.—The text is that printed in the *Appendix to Hymns Ancient and Modern,* 1868, and ever since the standard. An autograph copy of the hymn in the writer's possession reads, in the second line of the second verse, "Satan's legions flee."

THE STORY OF THE HYMN

This marching hymn was written in England just at the time when in our own country the sad strife of the Civil War had drawn to a close. And it is not unlikely that the new soldier-spirit left in the hearts of young and old Americans by the four years of the Civil War has had something to do with the marked popularity gained by this and other military hymns. An influence of the same sort can be seen plainly in American hymn books published after the close of the Revolution of 1776.

The Rev. Sabine Baring-Gould wrote the hymn while curate of a Yorkshire parish, and in a recent interview he has given an account of its origin. "It was written," he says, "in a very simple fashion, without a thought of publication. Whitmonday is a great day for school festivals in Yorkshire, and one Whitmonday it was arranged that our school should join its forces with that of a neighboring village. I wanted the children to sing when marching from one village to the other, but I couldn't think of anything quite suitable, so I sat up at night resolved to write something myself. 'Onward, Christian Soldiers' was the result. It was written in great haste, and I am afraid some of the rhymes are faulty. Certainly nothing has surprised me more than its great popularity." The hymn was written to be sung to a well-known tune by Haydn, which has been much used in American churches; so much used, indeed, that it became worn out.

"Onward, Christian Soldiers" was written in 1865. That same year it was printed in a periodical, *The Church Times.* As early as 1868 it was given a place in the *Appendix to Hymns Ancient and Modern,* thus securing a sponsor of the most influential kind. This was at a time when the Protestant Episcopal Church in the United States was restive under its old hymn book, and feeling its way toward something better. Eager eyes had already turned towards *Hymns Ancient and Modern.* Its very name pleased the growing party who were seeking "primitive" paths, while the High Church doctrine of its hymns and the ecclesiastical tone of the new "Anglican school" of music it represented, won their hearts completely. A reprint of *Hymns Ancient and Modern* and its new *Appendix* appeared at Philadelphia in 1869, with the imprint of the Lippincotts. In this "Onward, Christian Soldiers" appeared for the first time, probably, in this country. During the year following the Rev. Charles L. Hutchins included it in his *Church Hymnal,* originally planned for use in St. Paul's Cathedral, Buffalo, New York. In 1871 it appeared in the draft of the new hymnal laid before the General Convention of the Protestant Episcopal Church, becoming one of the authorized hymns of that Church. Into the church-worship of other denominations the hymn (like many other things that would once have seemed alien) gradually worked its way by first becoming familiar in the freer atmosphere of the Sunday-schools. The hymn was not included in the authorized *Presbyterian Hymnal* of 1874, although the compilers of that book made large use of *Hymns Ancient and Modern.* The rival *Hymns and Songs of Praise,* by Drs. Hitchcock and Schaff, published that same year, did, however, include it.

What proved a most effective letter of introduction for the hymn, and has secured its continued general use, was the appearance in *The Musical Times* for December, 1871, of the stirring tune written for it by Arthur S. Sullivan, to which it has been wedded ever since. At the present time it is unquestionably the most popular and often-used of all processional hymns. If it should ever drop out of use, that result would probably come about through sheer weariness caused by over-repetition.

THE AUTHOR OF THE HYMN

In this hymn we have for the first time one by a living author. Mr. Baring-Gould is so many-sided a man, with such a variety of gifts and accomplishments, and he has done so much work of so many kinds, that he may be said to combine in himself the material for the make-up of at least two distinguished men. There is, therefore, an amusing fitness in his compound name, and in the fact that sometimes he is indexed among the B's for Baring, and sometimes among the G's for Gould.

Mr. Baring-Gould is now rector of the parish of Lew Trenchard, where his family has had its seat for nearly three hundred years. He is also squire and lord of the manor and a justice of the peace. He lives in Lew Trenchard Manor House, inherited with the family property at his father's death in 1872. His study is described as a long, low room, with a deep embrasured window overlooking a lovely view, and paneled in fine dark oak, with the rich carvings of the old English time. In this room works the remarkable man, who is not only squire and rector, but also theologian, historian, antiquarian, student of comparative religion, novelist, and poet. The amount of literary work done in this room, much of it requiring wide research, is no less than amazing. On religious subjects, besides many volumes of his sermons and devotional and practical writings, he has written a number of works of a more learned character. Of these, the bet known, perhaps, are, *The Lives of the Saints*, in fifteen volumes, and *The Origin and Development of Religious Belief*, in two. He has published many volumes dealing with manners and customs, legendary and folk lore, antiquities and out-of the-way information, of which he is himself a living encyclopedia. *Curious Myths of the Middle Ages, Legends of the Old Testament, Iceland, Its Scenes and its Sages, Curiosities of the Olden Times, The Songs of the West*, are but a few of the more familiar titles. And for some time it has been his custom to write a new novel every year. In England he is one of the most popular living novelists.

In all his work Mr. Baring-Gould has employed no secretaries or amanuenses. "The secret is simply that I stick to a task when I begin it," he once said. "For some years I have found it necessary to spend the winters abroad, and while I am in the south of France or in Rome I think out the work which I am going to do when I return home. Thus I build up the plot of a story, and it all shapes itself in my head, even the dialogue. I make a few notes, principally of the division of the chapters, and then, when I come back, it is simply a matter of writing it out."

When asked if he did not have to wait for inspiration, he replied with a quiet smile, "Inspiration is all moonshine in the sense in which you mean it. It would never do to wait from day to day for some moment which might seem favorable for work"; adding that he often did his best work when he felt the least desire to go on with it. His hymn writing is, of course, small in quantity beside the great volume of his other achievements, but it certainly does not lack what is called inspiration, whether waited for or worked for. He has written many carols and quite a number of hymns, all of which have fresh and striking qualities. Next to "Onward, Christian Soldiers," the lovely evening hymn for children, "Now the Day is Over" (*The Hymnal*, No. 692), and his translation, "Through the Night of Doubt and Sorrow" (*The Hymnal*, No. 418), are probably most often sung.

Mr. Baring-Gould was born at Exeter, January 28th, 1834. He was graduated from Clare College, Cambridge, in 1854. In 1864 he was ordained and became curate of Horbury, where he wrote our hymn. From 1867 he was Incumbent of Dalton, until Mr. Gladstone appointed him Rector of East Mersea, in 1871. The rectorate of Lew Trenchard is what in England is called a family living, and when in 1881 the last incumbent died, Mr. Baring-Gould, who was the patron of the living as well as lord of the manor, became also rector of the parish by his own appointment. It cannot be denied that he chose an able and hard-working man to fill the post.

X

NEARER, MY GOD, TO THEE

THE TEXT OF THE HYMN

1   Nearer, my God, to Thee,
        Nearer to Thee!
    E'en though it be a cross
        That raiseth me;
    Still all my song shall be,
    Nearer, my God, to Thee,
        Nearer to Thee!

2   Though like the wanderer,
        The sun gone down,
    Darkness be over me,
        My rest a stone;
    Yet in my dreams I'd be
    Nearer, my God, to Thee,
        Nearer to Thee!

3   There let the way appear,
        Steps unto heaven:
    All that Thou send'st to me
        In mercy given:
    Angels to beckon me
    Nearer, my God, to Thee,
        Nearer to Thee!

4   Then, with my waking thoughts
          Bright with Thy praise,
      Out of my stony griefs
          Bethel I'll raise:
      So by my woes to be
      Nearer, my God, to Thee,
          Nearer to Thee!

5   Or if on joyful wing
          Cleaving the sky,
      Sun, moon, and stars forgot,
          Upwards I fly.
      Still all my song shall be,
      Nearer, my God, to Thee,
          Nearer to Thee!

Sarah Flower Adams, 1841

NOTE.—The text is taken from W.J. Fox's *Hymns and Anthems*; with a single change, referred to under "Some Points for Discussion."

THE AUTHOR OF THE HYMN

In the year 1820 there came to Dalston, then a rural suburb of London, a little family composed of Benjamin Flower, a widower, and his two daughters, the younger of whom was afterward to write this hymn.

Something of a career lay behind Mr. Flower, then an elderly man. Unsuccessful in business speculations as a young man, he had become a travelling salesman on the continent. There he became an adherent of the French Republic, and in 1792 published a book on the French Constitution which was really an attack on that of England. He was selected to edit *The Cambridge Intelligencer*, an influential weekly of radical principles. Accused of libelling the Bishop of Llandaff, whose political conduct he had censured, he was sentenced to six months' imprisonment in Newgate with a fine of £100. He was visited in prison by Miss Eliza Gould, a lady who is said to have suffered for her own liberal principles, and shortly after his release he married her. They settled at Harlow in Essex, where Mr. Flower became a printer and where Mrs. Flower died in 1810. These facts of their father's career help us to understand the atmosphere in which the motherless girls grew up.

Both daughters had inherited their mother's delicate constitution, but both were talented to an unusual degree, and they attracted to the Dalston home many friends who afterward became distinguished. Among those were Harriet Martineau and Robert Browning, "the boy poet," as Eliza Flower calls him in her letters, who came often to discuss religious difficulties with her sister Sarah. Eliza, the elder, was a skillful musician with a remarkable gift for musical composition. Sarah, the younger of the sisters, was also musical, and possessed of a rich contralto voice, and was much given to singing songs in costume, with appropriate dramatic action. The elder sister always furnished the accompaniment, and sometimes the musical settings of these songs, in their domestic entertainments.

Sarah Flower was born at the Harlow home on February 22nd, 1805. She had the dramatic instinct, and from childhood cherished the ambition of adopting the stage as a profession. She idealized the stage as an ally of the pulpit, and held that the life of an actress should be as high and noble as the great thoughts and actions she was called upon to express. In 1829 her father died, and in 1834 Sarah Flower was married to John Brydges Adams, a civil engineer and an ingenious inventor in the early days of railroad building. Her husband encouraged her dramatic ambition, and in 1837 she made her first public appearance, at the Richmond Theatre, as "Lady Macbeth." Her success was great enough to gain for her an engagement at the Bath Theatre. But her health gave way under the strain of public performances, and she suffered a seige of illness at Bath which at once put an end to all hope of a dramatic career.

Mrs. Adams determined to devote herself to literary work, for she had in addition a considerable literary gift. She wrote much for the *Monthly Repository*, but her most ambitious effort was "Vivia Perpetua – A Dramatic Poem," published in 1841. It tells the story of a young mother who suffered a martyr's death at Carthage, A.D. 203, for her faith in Christ. There is but little doubt that her own moral earnestness and intense feelings are set forth in the character of Vivia. The poem is often eloquent, but as a drama not well constructed, and it has taken no permanent place in literature. "The Royal Progress," a long poem in ballad metre, has met a like fate. Mrs. Adams's high ideals and ambitions led her to undertake tasks beyond her powers. Though ambitious to lead in the moral uplifting of the stage, even the ordinary routine of an actress's life was beyond her physical powers. And so her attempt to revive the poetical drama was quite as far beyond her intellectual powers. She had, however, a real gift for lyrical poetry. By her lyrics she retains a modest place in literature, and is chiefly remembered as the author of "Nearer, My God, to Thee."

Mrs. Adams is described by her friend, Mrs. Bridell Fox, as "tall and singularly beautiful, with noble and regular features; in manner gay and impulsive, her conversation witty and sparkling." The portrait here given is a facsimile of a slight sketch believed to have been made by Miss Margaret Gillies in 1834. Mrs. Adams seems to have made a deep impression upon the minds of those who knew her. They speak enthusiastically of her personal charm, and of her purity and high-mindedness. In his "Blue-Stocking Revels," the poet Leigh Hunt also pays tribute to her as "Mrs. Adams, rare mistress of though and of tears,"

Both of the sisters died while still in early life, and within less than two years of each other. Eliza died of consumption in December, 1846, and Sarah on August 14th, 1848; the death of the younger sister was probably ably hastened by the cares and anxiety occasioned by the long illness of the elder. At the funerals of both, hymns by Mrs. Adams were sung to music composed for them by her sister. One cannot avoid a feeling of regret that some foretaste of her usefulness and fame did not come to brighten the failing days of the author of "Nearer, My God, to Thee."

THE STORY OF THE HYMN

After the death of Mr. Flower, his daughters removed to Upper Clapton, a suburb of London, and there connected themselves with the religious society to which the gifted William Johnson Fox ministered, in South Place Chapel, Finsbury. Mr. Fox occupied and independent ecclesiastical position, though generally classed as a Unitarian. For the use of the congregation he prepared a collection of *Hymns and Anthems*, published in 1840 and 1841, in two parts. At his request Mrs. Adams wrote for the book thirteen original hymns and some translations. One of the hymns was "Nearer, My God, to Thee," and it first appeared in the second part of the book. Like most of Mrs. Adams's hymns it was set to music by her sister, and was often heard in the services at South Place Chapel.

"How she composed her hymns," says Mrs. Bridell Fox, "can hardly be stated. She certainly never had any idea of *composing* them. They were the spontaneous expression of some strong impulse of feeling of the moment; she was essentially a creature of impulse. Her translations would, of course, be an exception; also, perhaps, when she was driving words for music already in use in the chapel.

"Nearer, My God, to Thee" was not long in finding its way across the ocean. While Mr. Fox was compiling his hymn book for his London congregation, an American clergyman, somewhat like him in his religious views, the Rev. James Freeman Clarke, was organizing a new congregation in Boston as the Church of the Disciples. (It is the church described as the Church of the Galileans in Dr. Holmes's *Professor at the Breakfast Table*.) Mr. Clarke printed a new hymn book for it in 1844, including a number of hymns from Mr. Fox's book, a copy of which had been given to him by his friend Mr. Bakewell of Pittsburgh. Among these was "Nearer, My God, to Thee," and in 1846 Mr. Longfellow put the hymn into his *Book of Hymns*. It was some time, however, before it made its way into the orthodox Congregational churches. Henry Ward Beecher, who was never afraid of novelty, included it in the *Plymouth Collection* in 1855. But what started the hymn on its free course in America was the tune "Bethany," which Lowell Mason wrote for it and published in 1856. And when the hymn, set to this taking tune, appeared in 1859 in the wonderfully successful *Sabbath Hymn and Tune Book* of the professors at Andover Seminary, its general use became assured. By 1866 it had found its way into the authorized hymnal of the Presbyterian Church.

XI

WHEN I SURVEY THE WONDROUS CROSS

THE TEXT OF THE HYMN

1   When I survey the wondrous cross
       On which the Prince of glory died,
    My richest gain I count but loss,
       And pour contempt on all my pride.

2   Forbid it, Lord, that I should boast,
       Save in the death of Christ my God:
    All the vain things that charm me most,
       I sacrifice them to His blood.

3   See, from His head, His hands, His feet,
       Sorrow and love flow mingled down:
    Did e'er such love and sorrow meet,
       Or thorns compose so rich a crown?

4   Were the whole realm of nature mine,
       That were a present far too small;
    Love so amazing, so Divine,
       Demands my soul, my life, my all.

Rev. Isaac Watts, 1707

NOTE.—Four verses of the original five; for the omitted verse see under "Some Points for Discussion." The text is taken from the second edition of Dr. Watts's *Hymns and Spiritual Songs,* London, 1709.

THE STORY OF THE HYMN

While still a young man the Rev. Isaac Watts published in London, in 1707, a volume of *Hymns and Spiritual Songs*. It was intended to be used as a hymn book, but it was not a collection out of many authors, every hymn being composed by Watts himself.

In these days of hymn writing and hymn singing it is hard for us to feel how original and even daring his venture was. There had, of course, been writers of English hymns before Watts. But none of them had established a precedent or model to which he and others were expected to conform. He had to form his own ideal of what a hymn for congregational use should be. It was these hymns of Watts himself that were destined to become such a precedent to his successors; and that is what James Montgomery meant in calling him "the inventor of hymns in our language."

Watts had also to encourager an apparently impregnable prejudice in the churches against the use of praise of anything but metrical versions of the Psalms. This had been a matter of conscience ever since the Reformation, the idea being that the Psalms of the Bible were inspired by God to serve as the hymn book of His Church for all time, and that hymns were "merely human composures," unauthorized and unnecessary. Watts had ever the courage of his convictions, and he printed with his hymns and essay, not only denying that the Psalms were intended as the sole hymn book of the Christian Church, but arguing that it was the duty of the Church to make new hymns that should express Christian faith in the same degree that the Psalms had expressed Jewish faith.

Partly by his audacity, partly by the excellent of his hymns, partly also on account of people's weariness with the old Psalm versions, Watts won the day. In dissenting churches his hymns were put into use immediately. Their influence spread so widely and grew so great that in the end it completely overcame the prejudice against hymns of "human composure," not only in dissenting churches but in the Church of England the Church of Scotland. In America this prejudice against hymns was especially strong, but here, too, after much controversy, the influence of Watts prevailed. His *Hymns,* together with his later *Imitations of the Psalms,* became the familiar and loved hymn book of both the Presbyterian and Congregational Churches, excluding all besides for a considerable period. That the hymns of this innovator should thus become a badge and symbol of orthodoxy and conservatism in the churches that once disputed his way is an illustration of personal influence not easy to parallel.

The first edition of Watts's *Hymns* has become a very rare book, only two or three copies being known to exist. Out of these sold in London in December, 1901, for one hundred and forty pounds. This first edition contained in all two hundred and ten hymns, arranged in three books, together with several doxologies. In the third book, containing hymns to be used in the celebration of the Lord's Supper, "When I Survey the Wondrous Cross" appeared as number seven. Within two years Watts wrote one hundred and forty-four more, and added them in the second edition of 1709; at the same time making many alterations in the text of those printed at the earlier date.

Of the two hundred and ten hymns included in the first edition it is probable that the larger number were written by Watts during the years 1695 and 1696, both of which he spent at his father's house in preparation for his entrance into the ministry. There is in existence a letter from his brother Enoch, dated as early as March 1700, urging the speedy publication of the hymns for use in public worship. One of Dr. Watts's earlier biographers gives the following account of their origin: "Mr. John Morgan, a minister of very respectable character now living at Romsey, Hants, has sent me the following information: 'The occasion of the Doctor's hymns was this, as I had the account from his worthy fellow-laborer and colleague, the Rev. Mr. Price, in whose family I dwelt above fifty years ago. The hymns which were sung at the Dissenting meeting at Southampton were so little to the gust of Mr. Watts that he could not forbear complaining of them to his father. The father bid him try what he could do to mend the matter. He did, and had such success in his first essay that a second hymn was earnestly desired of him, and then a third, and fourth, etc., till in the process of time there was such a number of them as to make up a volume.'" This may be accepted as the traditional account of the origin of the hymns, and doubtless may be trusted as far as at least to show that they grew out of Watts's early dissatisfaction with the material available for congregational praise, and his determination to provide better material.

The hymns we are now studying can hardly be said to have a special history as apart from the others in Watts's epoch-making book. But there are several things that single out this hymn from among the rest. One is its extraordinary excellence. It is not only the best of all Watts's hymns, but it is placed by common consent among the greatest hymns in the language. Another is the wideness of its use. The greater part of Watts's hymns are left behind; this is sung in every branch of the English-speaking Church. Judged by the number of hymnals containing it, only one hymn is used more widely – Toplady's "Rock of Ages." Its greatest glory, however, is the part it has had in the experience of Christians. Only God can know how many living eyes it has inspired with the ideal of the cross of renunciation, how many dying eyes it has comforted with the vision of the cross of hope.

THE AUTHOR OF THE HYMN

Isaac Watts was born July 17th, 1674, at the English town of Southampton, where his father was deacon of a Congregational church. It was at a time when the laws against nonconformity to the state religion were still enforced with bitterness, and he was often carried in his mother's arms to the town jail, where she visited his father, imprisoned for conscience' sake. The accounts of Watts's childhood tell of a pale, underside child, asking those about him to "buy a book" before he could pronounce the words plainly, beginning Latin at four, and writing poetry at seven. Perhaps there is an element of exaggeration in such stories. The portraits of Dr. Watts in his ponderous eighteenth century wig make it hard enough to think of him as ever young, and these accounts do not much encourage one in that attempt.

After his school days at Southampton, a few friends, impressed by his diligence and abilities, offered to send him to one of the universities.

But the universities were not open to dissenters, and among these the young scholar had determined to abide. He entered the academy of the Rev. Thomas Rowe at Stoke Newington, and in 1693 was admitted to the church of which Mr. Rowe was pastor. At twenty he had completed the ordinary course of study, and had returned to his father's house, spending two years there in study and spiritual preparation for the ministry. Afterward he lived for several years with Sir John Hartopp as the tutor of his son, carrying forward his own studies at the same time.

On his twenty-fourth birthday Watts preached his first sermon. He became the assistant, and in 1702 was ordained the successor, of Dr. Isaac Chauncy, pastor of the Independent Church meeting in Mark Lane, London. Already, as Dr. Chauncy's assistant, he had been laid aside for several months by sickness, and soon after his ordination he was seized with a dangerous illness which left him so weak as to require an assistant of his own. From 1712 to 1716 he was again laid aside by a fever and its consequences, from which he never fully recovered. Happily he had the gift of making people love him. His church was always patient and sympathetic, and in his weakness and loneliness he was invited to the palatial home of Sir Thomas Abney, Theobalds, not far from London. Expecting to stay a week, he remained in the family for the rest of his life, thirty-six years, a loved and honored guest. Here he continued his care of his church, preaching when able and engaging in literary work. Lady Abney watched over him with unremitting care, shielding him, so far as she could, from anxieties and troubles, until he died, after a long illness, November 25th, 1748.

"Few men," said the great Dr. Johnson, "have left behind such purity of character or such monuments of laborious piety." His published works cover many departments – geography, astronomy, philosophy, theology, practical religion, and poetry. In all these departments he was accomplished and useful. But his own estimate, that in completing his *Psalms and Hymns* he had produced his greatest work for the use of the Church, is undoubtedly true. Providence had a special mission for him in that department, and through it his name and influence must always endure.

XII

O STILL IN ACCENTS SWEET AND STRONG

THE TEXT OF THE HYMN

1   O still in accents sweet and strong
        Sounds forth the ancient word,
    "More reapers for white harvest fields,
        More laborers for the Lord."

2   We hear the call; in dreams no more
        In selfish ease we lie,
    But, girded for our Father's work,
        Go forth beneath His sky.

3   Where prophets' word, and martyrs' blood,
        And prayers of saints were sown,
    We, to their labors entering in,
        Would reap where they have strown.

4   O Thou whose call our hearts has stirred,
        To do Thy will we come;
    Thrust in our sickles at Thy word,
        And hear our harvest home.

Rev. Samuel Longfellow, 1864

NOTE.—The text is taken from *Hymns of the Spirit*, which Mr. Longfellow compiled, in conjunction with his friend, the Rev. Samuel Johnson.

THE AUTHOR OF THE HYMN

In all the editions of the poetical works of Henry W. Longfellow there is found among the earlier poems one entitled "Hymn for my Brother's Ordination." It is this brother, the Rev. Samuel Longfellow, who is the author of the hymn now to be studied.

The Longfellow family lived in Portland, Maine. The father was a greatly respected lawyer there, and surrounded his family with comfort and refinement. The square brick house in which they lived, and in which Samuel, the younger of the brothers, was born June 18th, 1819, is still standing, though now in the business quarter of the town.

Just as the older brother gravitated naturally toward a literary life, so the younger brother gravitated toward the ministry. From Harvard, where he was a classmate and close friend of Edward Everett Hale, he was graduated in 1839; and, after a few y ears spent in teaching and study, entered the divinity school of that university, being graduated in 1846. It was while a student there that he and another friend, Samuel Johnson, under took to compile a new hymn book for Unitarian churches – a somewhat audacious venture for two theological students. The book appeared in 1846, under the name of *The Book of Hymns*; though Theodore Parker, who was one of the first to use it in his services, was wont to call it "The Book of Sams."

The book was very remarkable for literary merit. It broke away from the old tradition of dull and heavy hymns, and brought before the churches many that were fresh and beautiful. Among these were "Lead, Kindly Light," which the editors had found in a newspaper, and many of the hymns of Mr. Whittier and of other American writers. The book had a great influence far beyond the bounds of those who had shared the peculiar religious beliefs of its young editors.

Mr. Longfellow was ordained as a Unitarian minister in 1848, and became pastor at Fall River, Massachusetts, and afterward at Brooklyn. After a long interval Mr. Longfellow in 1878 began his last pastorate at the Unitarian Church of Germantown, a Philadelphia suburb. The whole period of his settled pastoral life was less than fifteen years. Together with a lack of physical robustness, there was a craving for the quiet life and a shrinking from formality and routine. Resigning his charge in 1882, he took up his residence in the famous "Craigie House" in Cambridge that had been the home of his brother, the poet; giving up his closing years to writing that brother's biography. Mr. Longfellow died October 3rd, 1892, and was buried from the old home at Portland.

No brothers were ever more devoted than these. But at the same time there are disadvantages in being the younger brother of a famous poet; and while Samuel Longfellow had the poetic temperament, and was not lacking in the poetic gift, and was a prominent man in Unitarian circles, it has happened nevertheless that the light of his fame has burned, and always must burn, with a paler flame, because nature set it alongside of the far brighter blaze of his brother's renown. To most readers Samuel Longfellow is known simply as the poet's brother and biographer. Yet he was in all respects a man worth knowing for his own sake: "full of enthusiasm of the quiet, deep, interior kind; worshipful, devout, reverent; a deep believer in the human heart, in its affections; having a perfect trust in the majesty of conscience, a supreme trust in God and in the laws of the world; a man thoroughly well informed, used to the best people, used to the best books and the best music, with the soul of a poet in him and the heart of a saint; a man of deeply, earnestly consecrated will; simple as a little child; perpetually singing little ditties as he went about in the world, humming his little heart-songs as he went about in the street, wherever you met him." "A very perfit gentil knight" was the old phrase applied to him by Colonel Higginson.

And yet this sympathetic pastor, this sunny-hearted gentleman, all the motives of whose life were high and spiritual, who lived and did his work within a perpetual atmosphere of calm and sweet serenity, came gradually to assume an attitude toward Christianity that only the gentleness of his heart and his pervading charity saved from being obstructive. Mr. Longfellow's religious inheritance was that of the temper and beliefs of the older Unitarianism, and with this point of view the hymn book of his seminary days corresponds. His point of view appears in his choice of hymns, which freely recognize the supernatural character of Christ. It appears in the very grouping of the hymns under such main heads as "Jesus Christ," "Communion Hymns," "Christianity and the Christian Life." How far that point of view was left behind as Mr. Longfellow's life advanced is revealed nowhere more plainly than in a second hymn book compiled in the early sixties by the same two life-long friends, and published at Boston in 1864 as *Hymns of the Spirit.* From this later book all hymns "which attributed a peculiar quality and special authority to Christianity, and recognized a supernatural element in the personality of Jesus," were excluded. Even the hymn, "Christ to the Young Man Said," composed for his ordination by his famous brother was omitted because "he would not by that one name disturb the simplicity of his faith in the one Source of the soul's higher life." The Communion Hymns were left out, as the rite itself had disappeared from Mr. Longfellow's ministry. "Christianity" appears only as the heading of a group of seventeen hymns out of a total of seven hundred and seventeen. The viewpoint of the book was that which its editor had declared his own to be – that of universal religion of which Christianity was only an illustration, of theism as distinguished from Christianity.

If we are to take Mr. Longfellow at his word, and regard him as a theist rather than a Christian, there remains at least the satisfaction of recognizing the striking moral coincidences between his conception of universal religion and our own of Christianity. There remains the greater satisfaction of finding his character and ways so many illustrations of what Christianity has done for life. But among those who care for Mr. Longfellow's hymns there will be very many who prefer to think of this free spirit as poet rather than theologian. For the latter office he was indeed hardly qualified by either his mental bent or his habits of study. His was a mind of the sentimental cast, which sincerely loved truth and sought to find it, but in reality rejoiced more in a sense of unfettered freedom in the search itself than in any logical coherence of the beliefs that rewarded the search.

THE STORY OF THE HYMN

Mr. Longfellow wrote many hymns, most of which were included in *Hymns of the Spirit*. This hymn, beautiful and heartfelt as it is, has no striking features in its history. There is no account of its origin anywhere printed, and those who have written of it have simply said that it was composed for *Hymns of the Spirit* in 1864. The present writer, however, has in his possession an autograph letter of Mr. Longfellow's in which he states that "the hymn was originally written to be sung by a class graduating from the divinity school at Cambridge." He does not say in what year, and most probably did not remember, since his niece, who published a volume of hymns after his death, was not able to give the date of this one.

The hymn is becoming very popular in this country; abroad it is less used than Mr. Longfellow's beautiful evening hymn, "Again, as Evening's Shadow Falls," and his "Holy Spirit, Truth Divine" (*The Hymnal*, Nos. 22, 279). It takes a great many years for a hymn to get into general use throughout all English-speaking countries, and very few hymns attain such an honor. Whether this or any of Mr. Longfellow's hymns shall gain such a distinction can hardly be foretold.

XIII

JESUS CHRIST IS RISEN TO-DAY

THE TEXT OF THE HYMN

1   Jesus Christ is risen to-day,
     Our triumphant holy day,
     Who did once, upon the cross,
     Suffer to redeem our loss.
              Alleluia!

2   Hymns of praise then let us sing
     Unto Christ our heavenly King
     Who endured the cross and grave,
     Sinners to redeem and save.
              Alleluia!

3   But the pains which He endured
     Our salvation have procured;
     Now above the sky He's King,
     Where the angels ever sing.
              Alleluia!

4   Sing we to our God above
     Praise eternal as His love;
     Praise Him, all ye heavenly host,
     Father, Son, and Holy Ghost.
              Alleluia!

                        [a composite hymn]

NOTE.—The text is that printed in connection with early nineteenth century issues of Tate and Brady's *Psalms,* except that some (possibly all) of these issue read "hath" instead of "have" in the second line of the third verse; treating "pains" as a singular – a usage not without precedents.

THE STORY OF THE HYMN

There are a few familiar hymns which can best be described as gradual growths rather than as the creations of an author's mind. Some lines or verses have served for the nucleus of a hymn; these have been reshaped and added to time and again by the hands of successive editors, and in that way the hymn has attained the form we know. Poetry of a high order could not be made by such a process; but of these composite hymns the few that survive are such, to say the least of them, as have proved both serviceable and attractive. One of the best of them is our Easter hymn, apart from which the services of that day would hardly seem complete. And the history of its making is not without an interest of its own.

For the earliest form of the hymn we must go back to the fourteenth century. There is now in Munich a manuscript of that date containing an Easter carol in Latin, which reads as follows:—

> "Surrexit Christus hodie
> humano pro solomine. allel.
>
> Mortem qui passus corpore
> miserrimo pro homine. all.
>
> Mulieres ad tumulum
> dona ferunt aromatum. all.
>
> Album videntes angelum
> annunciantem gaudium: all.
>
> Discipulis hoc dicite,
> quod surrexit rext gloriæ. all.
>
> Paschali pleno gaudio
> benedicamus domino. all."

Other manuscripts of the same hymn exist, having additional verses. But we are specially concerned only with the first and second couplets, which are in all the manuscripts. For these two couplets proved to be the nucleus round which our hymn was to grow.

The first stage in the growth of the hymn is the turning of that Latin carol into English, four centuries later. The illustration here given is the facsimile of one page from a book printed in London, 1708, by J. Walsh. It had this title:—

"Lyra Davidica, or a Collection of Divine Songs and Hymns, partly New Composed, partly Translated from the High German and Latin Hymns; and set to easy and pleasant Tunes.'

Comparing the words in the facsimile with the first and second couplets of the Latin, it is readily seen that they are a translation of them, and not very different from the first verse of our present hymn. The remainder of the carol follows on the next page of the book, the whole reading as follows:—

> "Jesus Christ is Risen to day Halle-Halleluiah
> Our triumphant Holyday
> Who so lately on the Cross
> Suffer'd to redeem our loss.
>
> Hast ye females from your fright
> Take to Galilee your flight
> To his sad disciples say
> Jesus Christ is risen to day.
>
> In our Paschal joy and feast
> Let the Lord of life be blest
> Let the Holy Trine be prais'd
> And thankful hearts to heaven be rais'd."

We recognize also the "easy and pleasant tune," to which we still sing our Easter hymn, harmonized in two parts, the air and bass. The tune seems to make its first appearance in this book. Most likely it was composed for these words, but nobody knows. In many hymnals the statement still continues to be made that Dr. Worgan composed the tune, the fact that he was not yet born not seeming to make any difference. Nothing more is known of the translation than of the tune. Who wrote the English words, who edited the book, for whose use the book was intended – on none of these interesting questions is there any light whatever. But the fact remains that in 1708 we got a first verse and also a tune for our Easter hymn, though not as yet in just the form we know.

In 1749 or early in 1750 John Arnold, a musician living at Great Warley, in Essex, published the second edition of a collection of tunes called *The Compleat Psalmodist*. In this book the same tune appears again, but the hymn has been made over. Only the four lines of the translated carol from *Lyra Davidica* remain. These are altered, and there are now added two verses entirely new. The hymn in the earliest edition of this book seen by the present writer reads as follows:—

> "Jesus Christ is ris'n to Day. Halleluiah
> Our triumphant Holiday
> Who did once upon the Cross
> Suffer to redeem our Loss.

> "Hymns of praise let us sing
> Unto Christ our heav'nly King
> Who endur'd the Cross and Grave
> Sinners to redeem and save.

> "But the pain that he endur'd
> Our Salvation has procur'd
> Now above the Sky he's King
> Where the Angels ever sing."

This is substantially the modern form of the hymn. And here again there is no clue as to the authorship of the new verses.

Not much now remained to be done to the hymn. It needed a little polishing, and it needed to have a place made for it among the hymns sung in church. For these it waited until the beginning of the nineteenth century. At that time the Church of England was singing metrical versions of the Psalms. Tate and Brady's version was commonly bound in with the Prayer Books. Toward the close of the eighteenth century a few hymns had appeared at the end of the Psalms. How they got there is not known. It is thought the likely some printer, with the free ways of a dissenter, saw fit to fill up a few blank leaves left over at the end of a Prayer Book with hymns, and that he made his own selection. Certain it is that the hymns appeared there and that they appeared without authority. It is equally certain that they kept their place in later editions of the Prayer Book and were sung in the services. They not only stayed, but increased in number. Some time early in the nineteenth century, at a date not yet fixed, our Easter hymn was added to the little group. The changes in the text were not that many, and each change was for the better. This final form of the hymn corresponds to the first three verses as printed at the head of this Study.

In later years some editor, thinking that the hymn needed a conclusion, added a doxology by the Rev. Charles Wesley, originally printed in 1740. The doxology (the fourth verse) suits the hymn and may now be looked upon as part of it. And the story of the making of the hymn, like the hymn itself, ends with this doxology. It was a long evolution, a somewhat curious history. Perhaps its most curious feature, amounting to something almost like an air of mystery, is the veil of anonymity that is not once lifted through all the five hundred years. Many hands have wrought to bring the materials into shape, and of all these hands not one can be associated with a human name or presence.

The popularity of the hymn is readily explained. It appeared at t time when suitable Easter hymns were sadly lacking, already provided with a string melody. And both hymn and tune have kept their place because they express, somewhat quaintly but none the less fitly, the gratitude and gladness of the Christian heart in view of Christ's resurrection.

XIV

A MIGHTY FORTRESS IS OUR GOD

THE TEXT OF THE HYMN

1   A mighty Fortress is our God,
        A Bulwark never failing;
    Our Helper He amid the floor
        Of mortal ills prevailing:
    For still our ancient foe
    Doth seek to work us woe;
    His craft and power are great,
    And, armed with cruel hate,
        On earth not his equal.

2   Did we in our own strength confide,
        Our striving would be losing;
    Were not the right man on our side;
        The man God's own choosing:
    Dost ask who that may be?
    Christ Jesus, it is He;
    Lord Sabaoth His Name
    From age to age the same,
        And He must win the battle.

3   And though this world, with devils filled,
               Should threaten to undo us;
        We will not fear, for God hath willed
               His truth to triumph through us:
        The prince of darkness grim,—
        We tremble not for him;
        His rage we can endure,
        For lo! his doom is sure,
               One little word shall fell him.

4   That word above all earthly powers,
               No thanks to them, abideth;
        The Spirit and the gifts are ours
               Through Him who with us sideth:
        Let goods and kindred go,
        This mortal life also;
        The body they may kill:
        God's truth abideth still,
               His kingdom is for ever.

Rev. Martin Luther (about) 1528
Translated by Rev. Frederic Henry Hedge, 1850

NOTE.—The text is taken from Hedge and Huntington's *Hymns for the Church of Christ.*

THE STORY OF THE HYMN

The greatest scene of Luther's career was his brave stand before the Diet of Worms, on the 17th of April, 1521. It was on the way thither, when warned by Spalatin against entering the city, that Luther wrote back: "Were there as many devils in Worms as there are tiles on the roofs of the houses, I would go in." Perhaps the occurrence of this same sentiment in the third verse Luther's hymn, "Ein' Feste Burg ist Unser Gott," is what led so many writers to say that he hymn was also written on that journey o Worms. Picturesque as it may be thus to connect the great hymn with the great event, the claim is not supported by any actual evidence. Three years afterward, in 1524, Luther printed his earlier hymns, but this is not among them. One naturally concludes that it had not been written.

Six other dates and occasions for the origin of the hymn have been fixed upon, each of them with considerable confidence. No one could be more sure of anything than is the Merle d'Aubigné, the brilliant historian of the Reformation, that Luther wrote the hymn while with the Elector John of Saxony, who was on his way to the Diet of Augsburg in 1530. That writer pictures the very scene. "John," he says, "began his journey on the 3rd April, with one hundred and sixty horsemen, clad in rich scarlet cloaks, embroidered with gold. Every man was aware of the dangers that threatened the Elector, and hence many in his escort marched with downcast eyes and sinking hearts. But Luther, full of faith, revived the courage of his friends by composing, and singing with his fine voice that beautiful hymn, since become so famous: Ein' Feste Burg ist Unser Gott." Here again is a picturesque origin found for the hymn, but one improbable on its face, and contradicted by the fact that at the time referred to Luther's hymn had already appeared in print. Various monographs have been published advocating other dates and occasions. Undeterred by these, Scherer, the recent historian of German Literature, states with entire confidence that the hymn was written in October, 1527, at the approach of the plague. Luther's biographer, Julius Köstlin, in the later editions of the *Life*, accepts that date as probably correct. And with that probability we must rest. The actual evidence in the matter is the appearance of the hymn in print. Some years ago it was found in a mutilated copy of a Wittenberg hymn book of 1529; and more lately report was made of its discovery in an earlier issue, dating apparently from February, 1528. It was already set to the glorious tune, believed by many to be composed by Luther himself, to which it has been sung ever since. The best opinion of the present time is that not any of the tunes furnished by Luther were original compositions, but were rather drawn from sacred or popular sources. That of "Ein Feste Burg," it is claimed, was developed from an old Gregorian melody.

Such a hymn, with such a tune, spread quickly, as may well be believed; "quickly, as if the angels had been the carriers," one enthusiastic writer has said. But they were men and not angels who spread Luther's hymn of faith and courage from heart to heart and from lip to lip. It thrilled them like a trumpet blast, encouraging the faint-hearted and nerving the brave to fight the battle of the Lord. It was, as Heine said, the Marseillaise of the Reformation. It was sung at Augsburg during the Diet, and in all the churches of Saxony, often against the protest of the priest. It was sung in the streets; and, so heard, comforted the hearts of the Melanchthon, Jonas, and Cruciger, as they entered Weimar, when banished from Wittenberg in 1547. It was sung by poor Protestant emigrants on their way into exile, and by martyrs at their death. It is woven into the web of the history of Reformation times, and it became the true national hymn of Protestant Germany. Gustavus Adolphus ordered it sung by his army before the battle of Leipzig, in 1631, and on the field of that battle it was repeated, more than two centuries afterward, by the throng assembled at the jubilee of the Gustavus Adolphus Association. Again, it was the battle hymn of his army at Lützen, in 1632, in which the King was slain, but his army won the victory. It has had a part in countless celebrations commemorating the men and events of the Reformation; and its first line is engraved on the base of Luther's monument at Wittenberg. And it is dear still to the German people; one of the hymns lodged in their memories and hearts, ready for the occasion. An imperishable hymn! not published and artistically wrought, but rugged and strong like Luther himself, whose very words seem like deeds.

Among Luther's hymns (some thirty-six in all) this occupies the supreme place, because it is the fullest expression of what he was as a man and as a reformer. "It is a true picture of his simple faith in Christ, and of his immovable trust in God, his forgetfulness of self and entire consecration of his life and all that he held dear to that Saviour who, he doubted not, would speedily, gloriously, and for ever, triumph over Satan and all his hosts, by the word which he was the honored instrument once more to proclaim to the world."

THE TRANSLATOR OF THE HYMN

The translating of Luther's hymn began very early. His hymns seemed to the early Protestants like part of their confession of the new faith; and as Lutheran ideas spread into other countries, the hymns were translated, and sung by the people in their own tongues. In the English Reformation, however, they had no part. While an exile in Germany, toward the middle of the sixteenth century, Myles Coverdale came into contact with them, and made versions of a number, which he printed in his *Goostly Psalmes and Spirituall Songes*. He seems to have been more interested in Luther's tunes than in the words. The forty-sixty Psalm in his book is in the metre of "Ein' Feste Burg," but only the first four lines follow Luther's hymn. The first real translation into English is probably that contained in the *Lyra Davidica*, published in London in 1708, and, like the book itself, anonymous.

The next version appeared in *Psalmodica Germanica*, a book of translations of German hymns published at London in 1722, by John Christian Jacobi, who had charge of the Royal German Chapel at St. James's Palace. This interests us more, because a reprint of the book came from the press of Hugh Gaine in New York in 1756. It was the first hymnal used in Lutheran services in English in this country, and introduced "Ein' Feste Burg" here as an English hymn. This version was reprinted by Dr. Kunze, of New York, in his Lutheran hymn book of 1795. But in after years, both in England and this country, knowledge of the hymn was mostly confined to the Germans until Carlyle called attention to it in his now famous essay, "Luther's Psalm," printed in *Fraser's Magazine* for 1831. Since that date very many writers, both English and American, have attempted versions of the hymn; how many, it would be hard to say. The Rev. Dr. Bernard Pick has collected eighty different translations in a little book, but there are many more. Of these versions, some are poor enough; and of them all, only two have proved widely successful.

To translate a hymn into another language, and yet to preserve the spirit and the form of the original, is always a difficult task. But to do it in such a way that a foreign people shall love to *sing* the hymn in their own tongue is a feat of which one may be proud. One of the two successful versions is the translation made by Thomas Carlyle, and printed in his "Luther's Psalm" in 1831. Carlyle's understanding of Luther, and his own gift of downright speech, well fitted him for his undertaking. In many respects his is the best version of the hymn in English; and in Great Britain it is the one most generally sung, although some changes are made in it, in most cases, to fit it for such a use. The other successful translation is American. It was made by a Unitarian clergyman, the Rev. Frederic Henry Hedge, and first appeared in 1852, in the second edition of Dr. Furness's *Gems of German Verse*. A year later Dr. Hedge included it (just as it stands in *The Hymnal* and here) in *Hymns for the Church of Christ*.

The translator did his work well. His version is worthy to stand beside Carlyle's, and for church use as a hymn is probably the better of the two. It has become the accepted version of Luther's hymn in this country, and now finds a place in the great majority of recent American hymnals of the better kind. Perhaps we hardly realize that Luther's hymn is gradually becoming one of the standard hymns of the American Church. More than once in late years it has happened that classes in our colleges have adopted it by vote as their class hymn. To this growing appreciation of the hymn several things contribute. One is the growth of historical feeling, making more of historical associations. Another is the clear ring of faith in the hymn itself, never more appealing than now. Still another is the quality of the old chorale to which the words are set. But Dr. Hedge's great success in producing such a version as makes us feel that we are singing Luther's hymn itself, must also be placed high among the causes which are acclimating to the old German hymn.

Dr. Hedge was decidedly a man of mark in New England; a thinker and scholar of influence. His life is linked with Harvard University by close ties. His mother was the granddaughter of one of its presidents, and his father a professor there for over thirty years. He himself was born at Cambridge, December 12th, 1805, was graduated in arts by Harvard in 1825, and in divinity three years later. While still pastor of a church at Brookline, in 1857, he became Professor of Church History, and in 1872 Professor of German, in the university. This latter chair he held until 1881, and lived until August 21st, 1890.

Dr. Hedge reached manhood at a time when there was great intellectual unrest in New England, and much excitement on moral and religious questions. It culminated in what is generally called the Transcendental Movement for a more spiritual philosophy. Dr. Channing was probably the leader of this movement, but Dr. Hedge took a most active part in it. He was one of the founders of the Transcendental Club of Boston, and of its eccentric organ, *The Dial*. Dr. Hedge's particular share in this movement seems to have been to make known and expound the literature, and especially the philosophy, of Germany. Before going to Harvard he had spent several years as a student in Germany. These made him so familiar with the language that it became to him practically a second mother-tongue, and gave him a sympathy with German thought, of which he remained a student all his life. He published, in 1848, a large volume of *The Prose Writers of Germany*, which became a standard work; and by lectures, review articles, and books, did much to make the philosophers of Germany more welcome than they had been in New England.

This translation of Luther's hymn, therefore, was quite in line with Dr. Hedge's special work. For keeping his memory green in the world it is, no doubt, the most effective piece of work he ever did. It was a little piece of work. And yet nothing less than his own religious nature and strong religious feeling, his poetic temperament and gift for making verse, his familiarity with German and practiced skill in translating it – nothing less than all these things, combined in the one man, made success in that little piece of work possible.

Dr. Hedge's connection with the hymnody of the Church at large does not extend much beyond this contribution of his translation of the great Reformer's hymn. He holds an honorable place in the succession of American editors. In cooperation with the Rev. Frederick D. Huntington (then a Unitarian, afterward Bishop in the Protestant Episcopal Church) he prepared, and published in 1853 for use in Unitarian churches, the *Hymns for the Church of Christ* already referred to. It had, and deserved, much success, being of a high order both poetically and spiritually. The book was worth while, if only because it introduced to the churches that fine morning hymn, "Now, when the

Dusky Shades of Night, Retreating" (*The Hymnal*, No. 8). If, indeed, the editors had been careful to make a note of the authorship or source of that hymn (now apparently irrevocably lost) their service would still be more appreciated by the curious. Dr. Hedge contributed a number of original hymns to the book. One of the bets is that beginning, "Beneath Thine hammer, Lord, I lie." Another, which sets forth the cross as the sign of Christ's leadership, beginning, "'Twas the day when God's Anointed," has particular merit, judged from its own point of view. But none of Dr. Hedge's original hymns has come into more than a limited use, even within strictly Unitarian circles. For that reason any inquiry into his theological position and views is less pertinent. It is just as well, since it would be difficult to classify him as connected with any special school of thought. He distrusted system and cared little for logical consistency. His position was altogether independent and some-times undefined. Certainly he hewed a path far beyond the conven-tions of Christian theology. What we have to be especially grateful for is the undisturbed reflection he gave forth of the spirit and words of Luther's hymn.

XV

ABIDE WITH ME: FAST FALLS THE EVENTIDE

THE TEXT OF THE HYMN

1   Abide with me: fast falls the eventide;
The darkness deepens; Lord, with me abide:
When other helpers fail, and comforts flee,
Help of the helpless, O abide with me.

2   Swift to its close ebbs out life's little day;
Earth's joys grow dim, its glories pass away
Change and decay in all around I see;
O Thou who changest not, abide with me.

3   I need Thy presence every passing hour;
Ills have no weight, and tears no bitterness.
Where is death's sting? where, grave, thy victory?
I triumph still, if Thou abide with me.

4   Hold Thou Thy cross before my closing eyes;
Shine through the gloom, and point me to the skies:
Heaven's morning breaks, and earth's vain shadows flee:
In life, in death, O Lord, abide with me.

Rev. Henry Francis Lyte, 1847

NOTE. – Five verses of the original eight (see under "Some Points for Discussion").

THE STORY OF THE HYMN

The darkness that deepens in this hymn is the shadow of death creeping over the poet himself, whose last song it was. The Rev. Henry Francis Lyte, who was pastor as well as poet, had been for nearly twenty-five years in charge of the district church at Lower Brixham on the shores of Torbay, England. Originally a little fishing village, it had grown into a somewhat disorderly and immoral district, with a rough and uneducated population. It seems a strange post for a gentle poet, but Mr. Lyte exerted a great influence over the sailors and fishermen, for whom he wrote songs, as well as hymns for their children in his schools. Never robust, he became year by year less fit for the heavy duties of the post, until the time came when he broke down utterly, and could live only by spending the winters in the warmer climate of Southern Europe. He had come home to spend the winter of 1847 with his church, but had lain extremely ill. Sunday, the 4th of September, was the last day of his permitted stay in England, and he shocked his family by announcing his intention to preach once more to his own people. "His weakness, and the possible danger attending the effort, were urged to prevent it; but in vain. He felt sure he should be enabled to fulfil his wish, and feared not for the result." He did preach, and although greatly exhausted, assisted at the celebration of the Holy Communion. In the evening of that same day he placed in the hands a member of his family the manuscript of the hymn "Abide with Me," together with a tune he had composed for it. On the following day he started for the South, but did not live to complete the journey. When within a few hours of Nice he was attacked by influenza, which soon developed alarming symptoms, and after some days of suffering he passed away.

It deepens the pathos of these circumstances to be told by Mr. Lyte's daughter (in her Memoir) that he was much distressed by the difficulties which had arisen among his people. A recent visible to Lower Brixham records a local tradition that a defection of some of his church workers is referred to in the words of the first verse, "When other helpers fail."

But the story of the hymn has a brighter side. It is pleasant to think of it in connection with another poem he left behind him, called "Declining Days." In this the poet asks himself why he should sigh at the thought of approaching death. He is described by one who loved him as a cheerful and unselfish invalid; but this touching poem shows, none the less, that he shared the regret common to invalids that his life had been frustrated by illness, and that he was only a burden to his friends. Death, he says, would seem even sweet could he think that in his narrow bead he should not be wholly mute or useless, but should help or heal some living heart by his verse:—

> "Some simple strain, some spirit-moving lay,
> Some sparklet of the Soul, that still might live
> When I was passed to clay!"

The poem closes with the prayer:—

> "O Thou! Whose touch can lend
> Life to the dead, Thy quick'ning grace supply,
> And grant me, swanlike, my last breath to spend
> In song that may not die!"

Not often are the prayers and longings of a disappointed heart so literally fulfilled. It was given to the poet to sing that swan-song that should not die. The Rev. Dr. George D. Baker, of Philadelphia, has told the present writer of meeting a young man at a church door in Nice one Sunday morning. They could not get in and walked together to another church, and after service went to visit Lyte's grave in the English cemetery. While they stood beside the grave in the English cemetery. While they stood beside the grave the young stranger became much affected as he told what the hymn had been to him. How far, indeed, is the author of such a hymn from being "mute or useless in his narrow bed"!

It would seem strange to us if "Abide with Me" were omitted from the hymn books. Buts its present position was not attained immediately, either in England or in this country. In 1855 Mr. Beecher, in his *Plymouth Collection*, put three verses at the service of American Congregationalists. In 1861 Dr. Henry A. Boardman, of Philadelphia, in his *Selection*, introduced the entire hymn to Presbyterians, especially of his own congregation. But he preceded by the notice: "[For reading only]." That notice reads curiously now. But he may have considered, as some still consider, the hymn too personal and intense for congregational use; or more likely, he knew of no tune that would carry the long lines. Indeed, the actual use of the hymn dates from the publication, that same year, of the now familiar tune in *Hymns Ancient and Modern*. After one of the meetings of the committee which compiled that book it was suddenly remembered that there was no tune for Hymn 27, "Abide with Me"; whereupon Dr. Monk, the musical editor (so he told a friend), sat down and composed in ten minutes the tune that has carried Hymn 27 to the ends of the earth.

THE AUTHOR OF THE HYMN

Mr. Lyte was born June 1st, 1793, near Kelso, Scotland, but was the son of a captain in the English army. Both parents died while he was a child, leaving him to struggle for a liberal education. Several prizes for poems gained at Trinity College, Dublin, were a welcome addition to his slender income, which he also supplemented by teaching; and he was graduated in 1814. He began the study of medicine, but in 1815 was ordained to the ministry in the Church of England.

His first charge was "a dreary Irish curacy," within seven miles of the town of Wexford – "Remote from towns, in almost perfect seclusion, giving myself up to the duties of my situation, writing my sermons, visiting my sick, catechizing my children, without other companions than my flute, my pen, and my books."

While there he had a strange spiritual experience. He was called in during the last illness of a neighboring clergyman, who he attended for some weeks. The clergyman, Mr. Lyte tells us, bore the highest character for benevolence, piety, and good sense. But his last days had brought distress and not peace, and he spent them in reviewing anxiously his own spiritual condition and grounds for hope. The sick man insisted upon going into an examination of the evidences for a future state, for the trustworthiness of the Scriptures as a revelation from God, and finally of the means by which a happy eternity was to be attained. "My blood almost curdled," Mr. Lyte writes, "to hear the dying man declare and prove, with irrefutable clearness, that both he and I had been utterly mistaken in the means we had adopted for ourselves, and recommended to others, if the explanatory epistles of St. Paul were to be taken in their plain and literal sense. You can hardly perhaps conceive the effect of all this, proceeding from such a man, in such a situation." The dying man found peace, and Mr. Lyte went forth a changed man, with a new spirit within him and a new message on his lips.

The strain of these weeks, with subsequent labors, proved too great for his strength. He became very ill, and was threatened with consumption – a shadow from which his after life was never to be free. He traveled on the continent, and on h is return, "after being jostled from one curacy to another," he settled down to work in a Cornwall village. Here he married, and soon after moved into the quiet country near Lymington, where he wrote many of his poems, and the *Tales on the Lord's* which Christopher North liked so well. In 1823 Mr. Lyte took charge of the district church at Lower Brixham, where he was to do the great work of his ministry. This charged he retained to his death, which occurred near Nice, France, on November 20th, 1847.

"A simple marble cross in the English cemetery at Nice fitly marks the last resting-place of one whose highest honor and desire in active life had been to exalt the Cross; who meekly bore the Cross through years of suffering, and who, trusting in the merits of his Blessed Saviour's Cross and Passion alone, calmly resigned his mortal life, in the sure and certain hope of a glorious immortality." With such words Mrs. Hogg brings to a close the Memoir of her father which she prefixed to the volume of his literary Remains.

Mr. Lyte's position as a hymn writer is a very high one. An earlier hymn, "Jesus, I my Cross Have Taken" (*The Hymnal*, No. 356), has been in the past even more used than this. Many other excellent hymns have been taken from his *Spirit of the Psalms*, a book originally printed in 1834 for the use of his own congregation. His miscellaneous poems are of much less important, and rarely reveal the creative touch of that imagination. One of them, "On a Naval Officer Buried in the Atlantic," was set to music by Sir Arthur Sullivan. As recently as 1868 a volume of Lyte's *Miscellaneous Poems* was reprinted in London, with a prefatory notice of "a continual demand for" them. The demand even then was perhaps less the call for specific poems of his than a curiosity to see what else the author of such hymns had written. But in the hymns lay his strength. It is distinction enough for one man to have written "Abide with Me."

XVI

GOD BLESS OUR NATIVE LAND

THE TEXT OF THE HYMN

1   God bless our native land;
Firm may she ever stand
Through storm and night:
    When the wild tempests rave,
Ruler of wind and wave,
Do Thou our country save
    By Thy great might.

2   For her our prayer shall rise
To God, above the skies;
    On Him we wait;
Thou who art ever nigh,
Guarding with watchful eye,
To Thee aloud we cry,
    God save the State

[The first five lines are here attributed to the
Rev. Charles Timothy Brooks as author or translator, (about)
1832-35; the remainder to Dr. John Sullivan Dwight, (about) 1844]

NOTE.–Of this hymn there can be no authoritative text. That here
printed is taken from Lowell Mason's *The Psaltery,* 1845. Two earlier
texts are quoted in the Study.

THE STORY OF THE HYMN

The one thing about this little hymn that seems certain is its excellence. And its excellence is not lessened by the fact that the hymn is cosmopolitan. It claims, indeed, to be translated from the German. Whether or not that is so, all who speak English, be they American or British, can sing it side by side. The meaning of the hymn is plain to all who love their native land. The authorship of the hymn is much less certain, and has all the interest of a puzzle.

(1) *Mrs. Henshaw's Claim.* – One day, in 1895, the writers saw, on a friend's table at Germantown, a little book of poems by Sarah E. Henshaw. Turning the leaves, his eye caught his hymn printed among the other poems of that lady as her own. Greatly surprised, he inquired of his friend who she was. He learned that she was a lady of high character, of New England lineage, who had lately died in California, and was the true author of this hymn. The writer at once started an investigation. He secured from Mrs. Henshaw's family a copy of a letter in which she had made her own statement of her claim as follows: "I wrote the verses just after the fall of Fort Sumter. I was then living in Illinois. I learned from the papers that the Rhode Island volunteers had gone through to the front, singing 'John Brown's Body,' and that Governor Buckingham had put the organization of our Connecticut regiments in charge of my uncle, General Dan. Tayler. With a heart on fire, and desirous that the Connecticut soldiers should also have something to sing, I wrote the verses in question. That everyone might know the music, I wrote them for the air 'God Save the King.' I sent them by post to may uncle with much hesitation, because he would probably think it all nonsense. Neither did I attach my name to the verses: I wrote at the caption, 'By a daughter of Connecticut.' I kept no copy, sent them to no publisher, heard nothing of then, took it for granted that my uncle had thrown them aside.

"After the war I moved out here [Oakland]. I drove down the street one Fourth of July to hear the schoolchildren sing. They sang my verses – *those* verses! I looked at the programme; there were the lines. 'Why! *I* wrote that!' I explained to [a friend'. As I wrote them, the poem contained several verses. Here were only two. But I was glad to get t hem. They were the first and the last. In writing them, I felt much dissatisfied with the last line of the last verse, viz.: 'God save the State'; and had earnestly cast about without avail for a stronger climax to match my rhyme. But here it was, just the same. I smiled at the recollection, as I carefully put the programme into my reticule."

(2) *Mr. Brooks's Claim.* – Mrs. Henshaw's letter was written to the Rev. Charles W. Wendte. Now it happened that Mr. Wendte had been the friend of the Rev. Charles T. Brooks, a poet and translator of much ability, pastor for many years of a Unitarian church at Newport. While sympathizing with Mrs. Henshaw's wish to establish her authorship, Mr. Wendte writes her: "My dear old friend, Mr. Brooks, whose memoir I wrote, called it his. He wrote so much that it is not at all unlikely he was wrong."

Mr. Brooks certainly claimed the hymn. In 1875 his friend Dr. Putnam printed the following statement, apparently by Mr. Brooks's authority: "Compilers and hymnologists have either marked 'God Bless Our Native Land' anonymous or else have attributed it to John S. Dwight. Mr. Brooks translated it from the German while he was a member of the Divinity School at Cambridge [1832-35]. It was shortly afterward altered in some of its lines by Mr. Dwight, and in its changed form was first introduced, it is supposed, into one of Lowell Mason's singing-books. Hence, doubtless, it came to be credited so widely to Mr. Dwight himself. We give the original translation of it by Mr. Brooks:—

> "'God bless our native land!
> Firm may she ever stand
>   Through storm and night!
> When the wild tempests rave,
> Ruler of wind and wave,
> Father Eternal, save
>   Us by thy might!

> "'Lo! Our hearts' prayers arise
> Into the upper skies,
> Regions of light!
> He who hath heard each sigh
> Watches each weeping eye:
> He is forever night,
> Venger of Right!'"

(3) *Dr. Dwight's Claim.*—"I hasten to say that the hymn, 'God Bless Our Native Land,' has been accredited for me for nearly fifty years, although I really had forgotten ever writing it." So answered, in 1893, Dr. John S. Dwight, the famous musical critic of Boston, when asked what light he could throw upon the matter. Dr. Dwight goes on to say: "Brooks reminded me once of our doing it piecemeal together. Certainly, it dates far back of Fort Sumter. About the year 1844 I translated many songs from a German song book for Lowell Mason's collection for our public schools – sometimes translating, sometimes making a stanza or two at first hand. I presume this was one of them. Brooks did the same thing for Dr. Mason. I did the work hastily and *cheaply*. I never thought of the song again.

Ten years earlier (1883) Dr. Dwight had written another letter, now in possession of the present writer, accompanying the autograph verse here reproduced. He explains that he transcribes and signs only this first verse of the hymn, "which I am pretty confident is mine." As to the second verse (as given in *The Hymnal* and here) he is less confident. "This also could have been made by me, but am not sure."

(4) *Mr. Hickson's Claim.* – As early as 1869 an English musician, Dr. William E. Hickson, had seen Dr. Dwight's name given as the author of "God Bless Our Native Land." He wrote to Mr. Sedgwick, the hymnologist, stating that he had written the hymn in 1836 as a new national anthem, and that it first appeared in his book called *The Singing Master,* published in the same year.

THE AUTHORS OF THE HYMN

We are now in a position to refer with some confidence to the joint authors of the hymn.

The Rev. Charles T. Brooks was born at Salem, Massachusetts, on June 20th, 1813. He was graduated by Harvard College in 1832, and by the Divinity School at Cambridge in 1835. His principal pastorate, at Newport, Rhode Island, began in 1837 and continued until 1871, when he resigned through failure of his sight and health. He died on June 14th, 1883.

Mr. Brooks was a poet and scholar, and also a diligent man of letters. The list of his works, original and translated, is a very long one, and their character is much as reflects honor upon their author's name. Gentle and retiring, he was greatly loved in life, though it is not likely that his work ever took hold of a very wide public. His translations of Goethe's "Faust" and of Richter's "Hesperus" and "Titan" are the best remembered of his productions. Of his hymns none has ever come into general use.

One of Mr. Brooks's most intimate friends, his classmate at Harvard and his co-laborer in several literary undertakings, was John S. Dwight. He was the son of Dr. John Dwight, of Boston, where he was born on May 13th, 1813. He was also graduated by Harvard in 1832, and by the Divinity School in 1836. His first and only pastoral charge was that of a little Unitarian congregation at Northampton, Massachusetts, and lasted only one year. At its close he quietly retired from the ministry. Bashful, sensitive, and lacking confidence in himself, he was hardly at home in the pulpit. He shrank too from any outward expression of religious feeling; in later years developing great dislike to church organization and methods, and ceasing to attend religious services. After the ministry came the years of his connection with the Brook Farm experiment, of which he was an active spirit.

But, wherever he was, the real enthusiasm of his nature was for music. He founded, in 1852, *Dwight's Journal of Music*, which, against great financial difficulties, he continued until 1881. It gave him a recognized position as the leader of Boston's musical interests, and through it and other labors he did great service to music as a branch of liberal culture.

Dr. Dwight (he became Doctor of Music) was of slender build and short stature. He was mild in manner, of a sweet and cheerful nature, and however shy, was "clubbable," being one of the famous Saturday Club. He was very positive in his opinions and uncompromising in maintaining his intellectual and aesthetic ideals. Dr. Dwight was singularly unfitted for the task of living. He met life in a spirit of helplessness that appealed greatly to his friends, and which, in spite of their efforts, kept him in a struggle with poverty all his days. He died at Boston on September 5th, 1893.

NOTE. – My friend, the Rev. James Mearns, of Buntingford, England, writes me of his discovery that this hymn is a rather free version of the first and third stanzas of a German hymn ("Gott segne Sachsenland"), by August Mahlmann, that was first printed in 1825.

XVII

FATHER OF MERCIES, IN THY WORD

THE TEXT OF THE HYMN

1   Father of mercies, in Thy word
        What endless glory shines;
    For ever be Thy Name adored
        For these celestial lines.

2   Here may the wretched sons of want
        Exhausted riches find;
    Riches above what earth can grant,
        And lasting as the mind.

3   Here the Redeemer's welcome voice
        Spreads heavenly peace around;
    And life and everlasting joys
        Attend the blissful sound.

4   Divine Instructor, gracious Lord,
        Be Thou for ever near;
    Teach me to love Thy sacred word,
        And view my Saviour there.

Anne Steele, 1760

NOTE.–Five verses of the original twelve. The text is taken from the *Poems* of Theodosia, vol. i.

THE STORY OF THE HYMN

If this hymn were to be taken alone, its story might be summed up very briefly. It is a leaf out of an invalid's spiritual diary, penned in the Baptist parsonage of an obscure English village. That leaf bears no date of composition, date being of but little account in the monotonous passage of such a life. The hymn first appeared in print in 1760 among the other poems of Miss Steele, but may have been written some years earlier; and it soon found the place in the hymn books which it has always kept.

This hymn has much of a story if taken in its historical connection with the whole body of Ms. Steele's hymns. Of these it is one of the best, and it has its share in the very conspicuous part they have played in the history of our hymnody.

Miss Steele's verses had long been familiar to her friends, but she was modest and reluctant to appear in print. It was by the advice and ever persuasion of others that at length she consented to publish them, and then without her name. In 1760 they appeared in two volumes, at London, as "Poems on Subjects Chiefly Devotional. By Theodosia." If one were now to take up the little brown calf books for the first time it would not occur to him that Theodosia was a poet of a high order. He would perceive, however, that many of the pieces were written in the simple metres then and used in hymns, and were composed with correctness and much tender feeling. He would probably conclude that they were intended to be sung, and might even point out a number as likely to succeed if put into the hymnals. This would be a judgment from the standpoint of our own time. To Miss Steele's friends and contemporaries it would have seemed faint praise indeed. They hailed her as a great light risen upon the horizon. She made an impression upon the Christian feeling of her time extraordinary both for its depth and for the wideness of its reach. Her hymns entered upon a career of popularity which we can hardly realize, but of which we must try to gain some idea.

Nine years after the appearance of her Poems two English Baptist clergymen, Dr. John Ash and Dr. Caleb Evans, published at Bristol a successful hymn book, containing in all four hundred and twelve hymns. Of these no less than sixty-two are by Miss Steele, and the preface has a special paragraph in her honor. After her death Dr. Evans printed in 1780 a new edition of her Poems, including a third volume she had made ready for the press. Even years later Dr. John Rippon published his *Selection*, which was destined to have great vogue among Baptists, and to supersede the Ash and Evans book. But even this contained forty-seven of Miss Steele's hymns. Dr. Rippon's book was often reprinted in the United States, and it extended Miss Steele's influence here. A simple fact will serve to show how widely her popularity spread and how long it lasted. The people of Trinity Church in Boston grew weary of singing the authorized Psalm-versions, and in 1801 the vestry ventured to print a hymn book for their private use. In this book of only one hundred and fifty-two hymns fifty-nine are Miss Steele's, and the preface explains that "if we have extracted more copiously from Mrs. Steele than from any other writer, we have done no more than we thought due to her poetical superiority, and to the ardent sprit of devotion which breathes in her compositions." Such a tribute from within the most exclusive of denominations, and from another country than her own, reveals something of the great influence of Miss Steele's hymns.

The three volumes of Theodosia's Poems were reprinted in Boston in 1808; and the hymns were reprinted once more in London as late as 1863 by Daniel Sedgwick, the hymnologist. But du ring the latter half of the nineteenth century the enthusiasm for what Dr. Evans called "those truly sublime composures" has been gradually cooling. Many of the hymns are still sung; some few are sung quite widely. But the latest American Baptist hymnal (*Sursum Corda*, 1898) contains but seven of the hymns of Theodosia in a total of eight hundred and fifty-six. Even that diminished number is somewhat larger than the average in recent hymnals.

Of Miss Steele's hymns still in use the one perhaps best known, and even loved for its tender grace, is that generally made to begin, "Father, whate'er of earthly bliss" (*The Hymnal*, No. 511). Another of her hymns, beginning, "Now I resolve with all my heart" (*The Hymnal*, No. 314), is by many associated with their first Communion. And it is quite possible that some who use the hymnals would welcome a larger number of Miss Steele's hymns than they find there. If these are possibly too inward, and pensive, for congregational use, it may well be that they have a further mission for private use, especially in cheering the sick room.

Miss Steele must always remain a figure of unique interest in hymnody. She is still the representative Baptist hymn writer. She was, too, the first of her sex to gain prominence in the hymn books. But her special preeminence is independent of her being either Baptist or woman: it lies in the extraordinary extent of the contribution she was permitted to make to the hymnody of the Church.

THE AUTHOR OF THE HYMN

Anne Steele was the daughter of William Steele, a successful timber merchant, who was at the same time pastor, without salary, of a Baptist church in the village of Broughton, England. Broughton lies about midway between the two cathedral towns of Salisbury and Winchester. Mr. Garrett Horder has described it as "one long straggling street of cottages, mostly thatched, with here and there a more pretentious house." In a quaint stone house in the centre of the village Anne was born in May, 1717, and lived for half a century. Anne's father had succeeded his own uncle in the pastorate at Broughton, and her mother was the daughter of another Baptist clergyman, so that Anne's religious heritage may be described as well within the limits of that faith and communion. When she was but three years old her mother died, and from her seventh year Anne was brought up by a stepmother, with much anxiety both for her spiritual and bodily health. Of physical health there seemed little prospect in a childhood threatened with consumption, and even that was lessened by a serious injury to her hip. This accident happened to her in 1835, within a few weeks after her father had broken his leg in a fall from his horse. The coincidence gave occasion for a quaint entry in the diary of Anne's stepmother (reported by Mr. Horder): "I desired our Heavenly Father to heal all our family's infirm limbs." The shadow of a greater grief fell on Miss Steele soon after, when the young man she was to marry was drowned while bathing in the river on the day before that appointed for the wedding.

Thus feeble in body and chastened in spirit, though never losing altogether her natural gift of cheerfulness, Miss Steele led a retired life confined almost exclusively to her own village. She never married, the title "Mrs.," so often given her in the older books being but a courtesy title, then often applied to single ladies. She had been a faithful member of her father's church since the age of fourteen, and as daughter of a village pastor she employed herself in many quiet ministries of service among the sick and afflicted about her. Her pleasures were in her friends and in the exercise of her poetical talents. While her writings have not unnaturally a tone of pensiveness and gentle patience, they show nowhere the least trace of bitterness of defeat. No one can read them without kindly regard for her beautiful spirit. In every experience her faith was supreme. It sustained her in the end through years when she was confined to her room in great bodily suffering, and it spoke to those about her in her last words: "I know that my Redeemer liveth." Miss Steele died in November, 1778, at the age of sixty-one, in her brother's house at Broughton, where she had gone at her father's death a few years before, and where she had received affectionate care. Her body was laid in Broughton churchyard, and on her tombstone are the words:—

> "Silent the lyre, and dumb the tuneful tongue,
> That sung on earth her great Redeemer's praise;
> But now in heaven she joins the angelic song,
> In more harmonious, more exalted lays."

No portrait of Miss Steele is known to the present writer, and from her sensitive modesty and seclusion it may perhaps be inferred that none was taken. Otherwise it would be hard to commend her good friend Dr. Evans in his choice of a frontpiece for the volume of her "Remains" which he published after her death. Only a sepulchral urn represents the poetess, to which a stilted female figure appeals with outstretched hands and the legend:—
"Forgive the wish that would have kept thee here."

XVIII

O DAY OF REST AND GLADNESS

THE TEXT OF THE HYMN

1   O day of rest and gladness,
      O day of joy and light,
O balm of care and sadness,
      Most beautiful, most bright;
On thee the high and lowly,
      Through ages joined in tune,
Sing Holy, Holy, Holy,
      To the great God Triune.

2   On thee, at the creation,
      The light first had its birth;
On thee, for our salvation,
      Chris rose from depths of earth;
On thee our Lord, victorious,
      The Spirit sent from heaven;
And thus on thee, most glorious,
      A triple light was given.

3   Thou art a port protected
      From storms that round us rise;
A garden intersected
      With streams of paradise;
Thou art a cooling fountain
      In life's dry, dreary sand;
From thee, like Pisgah's mountain,
      We view our promised land.

4   To-day on weary nations
    The heavenly manna falls:
To holy convocations
    The silver trumpet calls,
Where gospel light is glowing
    With pure and radiant beams,
And living water flowing
    With soul-refreshing streams.

5   New graces ever gaining
    From this our day of rest,
We reach the rest remaining
    To spirits of the blest.
To Holy Ghost be praises,
    To Father, and to Son;
The Church her voice upraises
    To Thee, blest three in One.

Rev. Christopher Wordsworth, 1862

NOTE.–Five verses of the original six: the omitted verse may be found under "Some Points for Discussion." The text is taken from the author's *Holy Year.*

THE AUTHOR OF THE HYMN

The Duke of Wellington said in 1827 of Dr. Wordsworth, the Master of Trinity College, "I consider him to be the happiest man in the kingdom"' and being asked why, the duke answered, "Because each of his three sons has this year got a university prize!" Of the three, Christopher, the youngest, born in 1807, was the author of this hymn. He was athletic as well as scholarly, and liked to tell how he "caught-out Manning" (the future Cardinal), at a cricket match. His career at Winchester and at Cambridge University was one of extraordinary extinction, and at its close he remained as Fellow of Trinity College and assistant tutor. Before he was thirty he was head-master of a great school, Harrow. The fourteen years of his mastership there may be called also a part of his education. He undertook a reformation of the school in manners and discipline with more earnestness than suavity, and though at the end of his anxious years there he left the school smaller than he found it, he took with him to a larger life new acquirements of tact and forbearance.

In 1844 Sir Robert Peel made him a Canon of Westminster Abbey. In that position he felt called upon to resist the appointment of Dr. Arthur Stanley as Dean with one of the "pamphlets" inevitable in English church controversy. Bitterly opposed as he was to the latitudinarianism for which Stanley stood, he tempered his earnestness with the courtesy he had learned at Harrow, and remained always on the best terms with the new Dean. From 1850 for nineteen years Canon Wordsworth was pastor of a country charge, which had the striking name of Stanford-in-the-Vale-cum-Goosey. Here he lied except when on duty at the Abbey, and here he accomplished an enormous amount of scholarly work. He had already gained a high position as churchman and scholar, writer and preacher, when in 1869 Mr. Disraeli appointed him Bishop of Lincoln. His administration of this large diocese was both strenuous and successful until his strength failed in old age. He died on March 21st, 1885.

Christopher Wordsworth's fame as man of letters and bishop is greater than as a writer of hymns. The mass of his published work is very great and its quality very high. His earlier work was in the lines of classical study, and his book on Greece itself has obtained something of the position of a "classic". But his two lifelong enthusiasms were for "Church Principles" and Holy Scripture. And his literary work, covering much ground in both these departments, and far beyond them, culminated in his massive and learned *Commentary on the Whole Bible.*

He was a man of very decided opinions, which he liked to establish when he could, and at least to express when he could do no more. In church matters he was for strict and unbending adherence to the Church of England pattern. He could be cordial with his Methodist neighbors, but he could not agree that their ministers should wear the title "Rev." He bore his part in many a controversy, never looking to see which side was the popular, but which was right. And if he struck stout blows for his somewhat narrow principles, it must also be said of him that he kept the friendship of his opponents. And that certainly is a good deal to say of him.

Bishop Wordsworth's opinions about hymns were just as decided as in other directions. He profoundly regretted that "Hymnology has been allowed to fall into the hands of persons who had little reverence for the Authority and Teaching of the Ancient Christian Church, and little acquaintance with Literature." "The consequence has been," he said, "that the popular Hymnology of this country has been too often disfigured by many compositions blemished by unsound doctrine, and even by familiar irreverence and rhapsodical fanaticism; or else it too often rambles with a glitter of tinsel imagery and verbal prettiness, or endeavors to charm the ear with a mere musical jingle of sweet sounds, not edifying the mind or warming the heart, nor ministering to the glory of Him to whom all Christian worship ought to be paid."

He thought, too, that our modern hymns were altogether too egotistical. They make too much of ourselves and our personal feelings, and not enough of God and His glory. He thought hymns of personal experience might do for private use. But for public use in church worship he did not approve of them. Church hymns should be churchly, expressing the worship of the congregation as a body and not as individuals. He would drop the pronouns "I" and "mine" from our hymns. We should forget ourselves and thank God for His great glory, and praise Him not for mercies to us as individuals, but to the whole company of faithful people. And especially he insisted that the great office and use of hymns was to set forth plainly and emphatically the teachings of the Scriptures and the Prayer Book. The hymns should teach the people the facts and doctrines of Christianity, and make "these glorious truths ... the subject of public praise and thanksgiving to Almighty God." His idea was that the hymns for each day for which the Prayer Book provided services should set forth the meaning and lesson of that which the day commemorated.

THE STORY OF THE HYMN

By way of carrying out his views in hymnody Bishop Wordsworth (while still Canon of Westminster) prepared a hymn book called *The Holy Year*, and published it in 1862. For this book he wrote one hundred and seventeen original hymns, and for a later edition ten more. All of them are good if looked at from the author's standpoint. But some things are best taught in prose, and when an effort is made to put them into verse the verse becomes prosy. And some of Bishop Wordsworth's hymns are prosaic and labored. He had, nevertheless, a vein of poetry in him (he was the nephew and biographer of Wordsworth, the great poet), and his best hymns are excellent, not only from his standpoint, but from any standpoint.

It cannot be said that *The Holy Year* in its entirety ever won much favor. Its title and its method of furnishing a hymn for each day and occasion for which the Prayer Book provided services at once challenged comparison with Keble's *Christian Year*. The inevitable results of such a comparison were once for all expressed by saying that *The Christian Year* was written by a poet with a strong theological bias, and *The Holy Year* was written by a theologian whose nature possessed many poetical elements and sympathies, but who is at times deficient in the accomplishment of verse. Mr. Keble himself, in a letter to Canon Wordsworth acknowledging receipt of a copy of *The Holy Year*, remarked that "to judge it properly it must take at least a year to read; for every hymn, of course, should be read on its own day – as a flower to be fully prized must be "studied *in situ*." It may be that the general reading of the book was more hasty. The general verdict certainly was that its use in worship would be calculated to correct some infelicities of praise by killing the spirit of song itself.

"O Day of Rest and Gladness" was number one in *The Holy Year*, appearing under the head of "Sunday," and certainly it was a real inspiration. Any one who loves the Lord's Day is pretty sure to love the hymn. It began to be copied into other hymn books almost immediately, and is now in general use in all the churches. It was introduced into this country in 1865 in *Songs for the Sanctuary*. Dr. Charles S.

Robinson, the editor of that book, stated that he found the hymn upon the cover of a religious tract in London. The words were set by him to Lowell Mason's tune, Mendebras, and the association of the two has been popular ever since.

A friend of Bishop Wordsworth has written down a reminiscence which brings us a little closer to the making of the hymn than merely reading a printed copy of it can do. His friend writes: "I was with him in the library when he put his arm in mine, saying, 'Come upstairs with me; the ladies are going to sing a hymn to encourage your labors for God's holy day.' We all then sang from the manuscript of this hymn. I was in raptures with it. It was some days before I knew it was written by himself."

XIX

TAKE MY LIFE, AND LET IT BE

THE TEXT OF THE HYMN

1   Take my life, and let it be
Consecrated, Lord, to Thee
Take my moments and my days;
Let them flow in ceaseless praise.

2   Take my hands, and let them move
At the impulse of Thy love.
Take my feet, and let them be
Swift and beautiful for Thee.

3   Take my voice, and let me sing,
Always, only, for my King.
Take my lips, and let them be
Filled with messages from Thee.

4   Take my silver and my gold;
Not a mite would I withhold.
Take my intellect, and use
Every power as Thou shalt choose.

5   Take my will, and make it Thine;
It shall be no longer mine.
Take my heart, it is Thine own;
It shall be Thy royal throne.

6   Take my love; my Lord, I pour
        At Thy feet its treasure-store
        Take myself, and I will be
        Ever, only, all for Thee

Frances Ridley Havergal, 1874

NOTE.–The text is that of Miss Havergal's *Songs of Grace and Glory* and of the authorized edition of her *Poetical Works*. As a poem she arranged it in couplets; as a hymn, in four-line verses.

THE STORY OF THE HYMN

The hymn of Frances Ridley Havergal records a deep experience in her own spiritual life, of the sort that most of us prefer to hide among the secrets of the soul. But Miss Havergal both spoke and wrote freely of the experience, and gave an account of the hymn's origin. It was her way to be perfectly outspoken about such matters, because she thought her frankness would prove helpful to others. And after her death her family, no doubt for the same reason, opened to the world the last reserves of her soul, and printed her most intimate letters and conversations. We are thus relieved of any sense of intrusion in our study of the hymn.

Toward the close of the year 1873 a little book that came into Miss Havergal's hands awakened within her great longings for unreached depths of spiritual experience and a fuller entrance into God's peace. It was not long before she received what she called "the blessing" that lifted her whole nature into sunshine, and threw an uninterrupted gladness over the remaining years of her life. "It was on Advent Sunday, December 2nd, 1873," she wrote to her sister, "I first saw clearly the blessedness of true consecration. It saw it as a flash of electric light, and what you *see*, you can never *unsee*. There must be full surrender before there can be full blessedness. God admits you by the one into the other." It is this full surrender of herself to which she then attained that is recorded and expressed in the hymn.

The hymn was written while on a visit to Arely House, on February 4th, 1874. Miss Havergal afterward gave the following account of the circumstances: "Perhaps you will be interested to know the origin of the consecration hymn, 'Take my life.' I went for a little visit of five days. There were ten persons in the house, some unconverted and long prayed for, some converted but not rejoicing Christians. He gave me the prayer, 'Lord, give me *all* in this house! And he just *did!* Before I left the house every one had got a blessing. The last night of my visit I was too happy to sleep, and passed most of the night in praise and renewal of my own consecration, and these little couplets formed themselves and chimed in my heart one after another, till they finished with, "*Ever,* ONLY, ALL for Thee!'"

Miss Havergal had her own characteristic way of writing hymns; and here again it will be best to let her speak for herself: "Writing is *praying* with me, for I never seem to write even a verse by myself, and feel like a little child writing; you know a child would look up at every sentence and say, 'And what shall I say next?' That is just what I do; I ask that at every line He would give me not merely thoughts and power, but also every *word,* even the very *rhymes* very often I have a most distinct and happy consciousness of direct answers."

THE AUTHOR OF THE HYMN

It has been said of Miss Havergal that she was born in an atmosphere of hymns. Her father, the Rev. William Henry Havergal, certainly wrote many, but is now best remembered for his services to church music and by his tunes "Evan," "Zoan," "Patmos," and others. She was baptized by another hymn writer, the Rev. John Cawood, author of "Hark! What Mean those Holy Voices? (*The Hymnal,* No. 169), and Almighty God, Thy Word is Cast" (*The Hymnal,* No. 74).

Miss Havergal was born in the rectory of the little English village of Astley, December 14th, 1836. The family removed to the city of Worcester in 1845, when her father became rector for one of its churches. The story of her child life there, its joys and griefs, and the beginnings of her work for others in the Sunday-school and "The

Flannel Petticoat Society," Miss Havergal herself has told in *The Four Happy Days*. She went away, first to an English school, under whose strong religious influences she began "to have conscious faith and hope in Christ," and afterward to a school in Germany.

With a real love of learning and an ambition to make the most of herself, she carried on her studies until she became a very accomplished woman. She was at home in Hebrew and Greek as well as in modern languages. In music she cultivated her special gift to such a degree that she was sought after as a solo singer in public concerts; and she became a brilliant performer on the piano. How she did it may be gathered from her poem "The Moonlight Sonata." Her own sense of power in her music and the delight of public applause enforced the advice from professional sources that she make music her career. She knew, too, that she held the pen of a ready writer and the promise of poetic achievement; and when there is added the influence upon her of marked social attentions evoked by the charm of her personality, and quickening her natural fondness for life and gayety, it will be readily understood that for a while the precise turn her life would take seemed somewhat problematical.

But it was never really in question. Love and service were the only ideals that could satisfy her nature, and to these she yielded herself so completely as to efface all other ambitions. Her gifts were thenceforward "Kept for the Master's use." She considered literal "Singing for Jesus" her most direct mission from Him, and after 1873 sang nothing but sacred music, and that only for spiritual purposes. Her great work was that of personal spiritual influence upon others, and was carried forward to the extreme limit of her strength by writing many leaflets and books of prose and poetry, by personal interviews, addresses, teaching, society work, and correspondence.

Many of her hymns were written for a hymn book, *Songs of Grace and Glory*, of which she was one of the editors. This was a large and carefully edited book, ardently evangelical in its point of view, but it took no permanent place in the Church of England. Many of Miss Havergal's poems were originally printed as leaflets. From time to time she collected them into volumes, of which *Ministry of Song* (1869), *Under the Surface* (1874), and *Loyal Responses* (1878), are the more important. After her death her complete poetical writings were gathered together and published by her sister. They made a bulky volume, and included, one would think, a great deal of verse which its author would not have considered worthy of appearing there. She also edited the *Psalmody* of her father, to whose memory she was devoted, and whose services to church music she lost no opportunity of magnifying.

Miss Havergal's ideals and methods in writing were not those of an artist. And, though her beautiful spirit is beyond criticism, it is only right to say that the cultivation of poetic art to the highest excellence (as in the case of Tennyson) may be pursued as conscientiously, and be as legitimate a consecration, as was the conscientious suppression of the art instinct in Miss Havergal's case. And while her hymns have been of great influence and won a wide use, it remains to be seen whether that influence shall be permanent, or was rather the personal influence of the devoted woman herself. For as the personal influence of a writer fades away, his or her work comes to be judged by what it is in itself. And one hardly feels that most of Miss Havergal's hymns are as good from a literary standpoint as she was capable of making them. Her "Golden Harps are Sounding" (*The Hymnal*, No. 702) is perhaps the best poetically, and seems too to have the promise of longest life. But many of her hymns have proved helpful to the spiritual life of others, and with that she would have been abundantly content.

Miss Havergal's later years were spent at Leamington, her last days at Caswell Bay, Swansea, Wales, where she had gone for rest. She had borne a full share of illnesses and suffering, and, though exceptionally sensitive to pain, had learned not only to carry forward her work under difficulties but also to find gladness in her infirmities. When informed of the dangerous turn of her last illness, she answered, "If I am going, it is too good to be true." Miss Havergal died in June 3rd, 1879, in the forty-third year of her age, and was buried in Astley churchyard beside her father and close to the church and home of her childhood. On her tombstone is carved, by her own desire, her favorite text: "The blood of Jesus Christ His Son cleanseth us from all sin."

127

XX

I WOULD NOT LIVE ALWAY; I ASK NOT TO STAY

THE TEXT OF THE HYMN

1   I would not live alway, I ask not to stay
Where storm after storm rises dark o'er the way;
The few lurid mornings that dawn on us here
Are enough for life's woes, full enough for its cheer

2   I would not live alway, thus fettered by sin;
Temptation without, and corruption within;
E'en the rapture of pardon is mingled with fears,
And the cup of thanksgiving with penitent tears.

3   I would not live alway; no, welcome the tomb;
Since Jesus hath lain there, I dread not its gloom;
There sweet be my rest, till He bid me arise
To hail Him in triumph descending the skies.

4   Who, who would live alway, away from his God,
Away from yon heaven, that blissful abode,
Where the rivers of pleasure flow o'er the bright plains,
And the noontide of glory eternally reigns;

5   Where the saints of all ages in harmony meet,
Their Saviour and brethren, transported, to greet;
While the anthems of rapture unceasingly roll,
And the smile of the Lord is the feast of the soul?

Rev. William Augustus Muhlenberg, (about) 1824

NOTE.—This text is taken from *Hymns of the Protestant Episcopal Church*, 1827. Other texts are referred to in "The Story of the Hymn."

THE STORY OF THE HYMN

A hymn so deeply tinged with melancholy as this illustrates two curious facts. One is that the saddest poetry is likely to be written by the youngest poets; the other, that the young appreciate such poetry more than the old. The brightness of youth has a vein of melancholy running through it, and the active imagination of youth forecasts the sorrows of life; while age, which has actually experienced them, likes to be as cheerful as it can. It need occasion no surprise, therefore, to learn that this hymn was written by the Rev. William Augustus Muhlenberg, somewhere in his twenties, and that, as he grew older, he grew to dislike it.

He came to dislike the hymn itself, thinking it did not truly represent either the joys or the opportunities of the earthly life, and that it was unduly impatient for the joys of heaven. To the end of his life Dr. Muhlenberg kept on writing new versions of the hymn in the hope (quite vain) that some one of them would replace the earlier text in popular favor. Dr. Philip Schaff's biographer describes a luncheon given by Dr. William Adams to Dr. Muhlenberg, at which Dr. Schaff remarked to him: "Your hymn, 'I Would Not Live Alway,' makes you immortal." Dr Muhlenberg protested, saying that he hoped to make changes in it to bring it nearer the spirit of the gospel. Dr. Adams interrupted the conversation with the remark, "Well, you may not be able to evangelize the hymn, but you cannot kill it."

Dr. Muhlenberg came also to dislike the popularity of the hymn, which from the very first was amazing. People would seek him out when busy with other things, "just to shake hands," as they said, "with the author of 'I Would Not Live Alway.'" He would be pointed out and introduced as "the author of the immortal hymn," etc. "One would think *that hymn* the one work of my life," he used to say.

The exact date of the hymn is uncertain. In his *Story of the Hymn* it is given in 1824. Several of the dates there are wrong; but this one is perhaps correct. In regard to the circumstances, or experience, out of which the hymn grew, there has been and continues to be a conflict of opinion. The tradition has always been that it was occasioned by a great personal disappointment suffered by its author. Dr. Muhlenberg was well aware of this tradition, and in his *Story of the Hymn* took occasion to contradict it in the following terms: "The legend that it was written on an occasion of private grief is a fancy." However conclusive this may seem, it has not concluded the matter. The Rev. Frederick M. Bird, in his essay on the Hymnology of the Protestant Episcopal Church, goes so far as to say that Dr. Muhlenberg's assertion "hardly agrees with the clear and minute recollections of persons of the highest character still living, and who knew the circumstances thoroughly." Two remarks seem to be suggested by this statement. One is that the persons referred to may have "known thoroughly" Dr. Muhlenberg's situation at the time and the reality of his private grief, and yet would not seem to have been in a position so good as his for knowing the exact connection, or lack of it, between the grief and the hymn. The other remark is that while we too, if we had enjoyed the privilege of knowing who the unnamed witnesses were, and of hearing of reading the exact words of their testimony, might have come to feel it more trustworthy than Dr. Muhlenberg's recollections after so many years; yet, in the absence of such opportunity, we feel ourselves bound by the explicit denial of the author himself. There will always, however, be many among the lovers of the hymn who believe the legend and not the assertion. The demand for a specifically romantic origin for every individual piece of verse for which one cares is unfailing. And in this case there is unhappily an apparent reality in the private grief in question, finding, as alleged, corroboration in the fact that Dr. Muhlenberg never married; there is even perhaps a coincidence in date between the sorrow and the hymn. Who but the author (and perhaps not he) could know how far his private grief had clouded the outlook of his muse upon time and the eternal?

For the next step in the history of the hymn, as related by Mr. Bird, the authority is more satisfying:—

"It was written at Lancaster, in a lady's album, and began,—

'I would not live alway. No, no, holy man.
Not a day, not an hour, should lengthen my span.'

In this shape it seems to have had six eight-line stanzas. The album was still extant in 1876, at Pottstown, Pa., and professed to contain the original manuscript. Said the owner's sister, 'It was an impromptu. He had no copy, and wanting it for some occasion, he sent for the album.' In 1826 he entrusted his copy to a friend, who called on him on the way from Harrisburg to Philadelphia, to carry the 'Episcopal Recorder' and in that paper it appeared June 3rd, 1826 (not 1824). For these facts we have the detailed statement of Dr. John B. Clemson, of Claymont, Del., the ambassador mentioned, who chances to have preserved that volume of the paper." And the present writer, in his turn, must rest upon the authority of Mr. Bird (which, indeed, is happily high); not having seen the album nor even chanced upon that number of *The Episcopal Recorder.*

Dr. Muhlenberg himself has told us how his poem first gained place as a hymn. From the paper, in which it was printed anonymously, it was adopted by a subcommittee among the hymns to be passed upon by the whole committee which then (1826) was engaged in preparing a hymn book for the Protestant Episcopal Church. When this hymn was proposed, "one of the members remarked that it was very sweet and pretty, but rather sentimental; upon which it was unanimously thrown out. Not suspected as the author, I voted against myself. That, I supposed, was the end it. The committee, which sat until late at night at the house of Bishop White, agreed upon their report to the Convention, and adjourned. But the next morning Dr. Onderdonk (who was not one of their number, but how, on invitation, had acted with the sub-committee, which, in fact, consisted of him and myself) called upon me to inquire what had been done. Upon my telling him that among the rejected hymns was this one of mine, he said, 'That will never do,' and went about among the members of the committee, soliciting them to restore the hymn in their report, which accordingly they did; so that to him is due the credit of giving it to the Church." It was copied almost at once into other books, and soon became one of the most popular of American hymns.

Ever since 1833 it has been associated with the melodious tune "Frederick," composed for it by Mr. George Kingsley, and printed as sheet music in that year. Kingsley belonged to the period of American psalmody when the performance of soloists and quartettes drowned the voice of congregations. The standard of church music did not differ materially from that of parlor music. Like the hymn itself his tune (even to the vignette on the title) reflects the religious fashion of the time. The two belong together. Several editors have attempted to put a newer tune in the place of Mr. Kingsley's. It was in vain, simply because words and melody both appeal to the same taste. They are not likely to be divorced, but to live or die together.

The history of the text is somewhat peculiar. The original, written in the album, seems to have been in six verses of eight lines each; as was also the first printed text in the *Recorder*. It was Dr. Onderdonk who selected and arranged the lines into four-line verses for the Episcopalian hymn book, Dr. Muhlenberg slightly revising them. So far as the public is concerned, this is the only text of the hymn. But in 1860, in a little collection of his poems, Dr. Muhlenberg printed a new version, and in a second edition, in the same year, added a postscript to that. In 1871, and again in 1876, he rewrote the hymn. It was not vanity but conscientiousness that inspired so much thought and labor; although these were quite in vain. The public loved the earlier version, and took no interest at all in the revisions. The autograph verses reproduced in this Study are from the version of 1871.

THE AUTHOR OF THE HYMN

Dr. Muhlenberg was born in Philadelphia, September 16th, 1796 and came of distinguished stock. His great grandfather was Dr. Henry M. Muhlenberg, founder of the Lutheran Church in America; his grandfather (Frederick A.) was Speaker of the House of Representatives in the First and Second Congresses during Washington's first administration. In his boyhood the Lutheran services were conducted in German, of which he was ignorant; and he drifted into the Episcopal Church, into whose ministry he entered in 1817. He was ordained by Bishop White, and for a while served as chaplain to the famous prelate.

In 1820 he became rector of the St. James Church, Lancaster, Pennsylvania. It was there he began his labors for a better church hymnody, publishing his *Church Poetry*, and doing much for that cause. While there he also conceived the idea of a school under church auspices, where education should be distinctly religious. Such a school he established at Flushing, Long Island, and gave to it fifteen years of enthusiastic toil. When circumstances compelled him to abandon it, he became in 1846 rector of a church in New York City founded by his sister, which he developed as a "free" church. Here he organized the first Protestant sisterhood, and established St. Luke's Hospital, in which, as pastor, he spent the last twenty years of his life, ministering to the suffering. In these later years he established the religious industrial community of St. Johnland on Long Island.

The great purposes of Dr. Muhlenberg's efforts may be summed up as the Christianizing of education, the reunion of all Christians in one Evangelical Catholic church, and the bettering of the lot of the poor. To these he consecrated his life, with his great gifts of originating and ministering. For these he spent his private fortune, of which he left behind more than enough to bury him. He was a prophet, and saw visions of a holier Church than any on the earth, more catholic of heart and more helpful of hand. He thought his own denomination called to lead the way, and committed to it his visions as a trust. Dr. Muhlenberg's ideals and influence constitute one of the great forces now at work in the development of the Protestant Episcopal Church. Of his spiritual greatness, his lovely personality, his saintliness, his utter abnegation of self-interest, it seems hardly possible to speak too warmly: "His long life was one stream of blessed charity." Dr Muhlenberg died at St. Luke's Hospital, April 8th, 1877, and was buried at St. Johnland.

XXI

O HELP US LORD; EACH HOUR OF NEED

THE TEXT OF THE HYMN

1 O help us, Lord; each hour of need
  Thy heavenly succor give:
 Help us in thought, and word, and deed,
  Each hour on earth we live.

2 O help us when our spirits bleed,
  With contrite anguish sore;
 And when our hearts are cold and dead,
  O help us, Lord, the more.

3 O help us, through the prayer of faith
  More firmly to believe;
 For still, the more servant hath,
  The more shall he receive.

4 If, strangers to Thy fold, we call,
  Imploring at Thy feet
 The crumbs that from Thy table fall,
  'Tis all we dare entreat.

5 But be it, Lord of mercy, all,
  So Thou wilt grant but this:
 The crumbs that from Thy table fall
  Are light, and life, and bliss.

6   O help us, Jesus, from on high;
        We know of no help but Thee:
      O help us so to live and die
        As Thine in heaven to be.

           Rev. Henry Hart Milman, 1827

NOTE.–The text is that published in Bishop Heber's *Hymns,* 1827.

THE STORY OF THE HYMN

It may be recalled that in our study of the hymn "From Greenland's Icy Mountains" reference was made to Bishop Heber's favorite project of a literary hymn book for the Church of England, a hymn book to contain only good poetry as well as good devotion. And now our study of this hymn, written by the Rev. Henry Hart Milman, brings us back to that project of his friend.

Heber had made a beginning on his book, at least as early as 1811, by writing some original hymns for it. But he never intended to follow the example of Dr. Watts and make the entire book consist of his own hymns. And we find him, in 1820, casting his eyes about the literary horizon to see what poets could be enlisted in his scheme.

There was no dearth of poets in those days. And it is likely that Heber knew most of them, for he had begun to write for the new *Quarterly Review* of Mr. Murray, the great London publisher, whose hospitable drawing-room was the common meeting ground of poets of the time. Keats, Shelley, and Byron were all alive in 1820, but no one then or now would be likely to think of them in connection with a hymn book. Crabbe was an old man, whose poetry lay behind him. Coleridge was capable of writing great hymns, but it was in vain to ask him to do any given thing at a given time. Keble at that time was actually writing *The Christian Year,* but the fact was known to very few. Montgomery, distinctively a hymn writer, would probably be passed over as out of sympathy with the Church of England. Wordsworth,

Scott, Campbell, Moore, Southey, and Milman were the six who remained, conspicuous and possibly available.

To at least three of these we know that Heber appealed to furnish hymns for his book. Scott and Southey both promised their aid. But both failed him, although some unnamed poet did send in contributions that were rejected as beneath the level of the book. To Milman, whom he greatly admired, Heber sent in 1820 an earnest request for hymns: "I know with what facility you write poetry, and all the world knows with what success you write religious poetry."

And Milman did not fail him. In May of the year following Heber alludes to three hymns already received from him, one of them the now familiar "Ride on, Ride on in Majesty" (*The Hymnal,* No. 214); saying "I rejoice to hear so good an account of the progress which your Saint [The Martyr of Antioch] is making towards her crown, and feel really grateful for the kindness which enables you, while so occupied, to recollect my hymn book. I have in the last month received some assistance from ————, which would once have pleased me well; but alas! your advent, Good Friday, and Palm Sunday hymns have spoilt me for all other attempts of the sort. There are several Sundays yet vacant, and a good many of the Saints' days. But I need not tell you that any of the other days will either carry double, or, if you prefer it, the compositions which now occupy them will 'contract their arms for you, and recede from as much of heaven' as you may require."

The hymn "O Help Us, Lord; Each Hour of Need" does not appear to have been in that first group, but very likely it was one of a second group acknowledged by Heber at the close of the same y ear. He writes to Milman: "You have indeed sent me a most powerful reinforcement to my projected hymn book. A few more such hymns and I shall neither need nor wait for the aid of Scott and Southey. Most sincerely, I have not seen any lines of the kind which more completely correspond to my ideas of what such compositions ought to be, or to the pan, the outline of which it has been my wish to fill up." At all events, we read of no more hymns from Milman in Heber's letters.

Milman contributed twelve hymns in all to the first edition of the book, which Bishop Heber was not to live to publish: and in that book, as put forth by the Bishop's widow in 1827, they first appeared in print. The book was immediately reprinted in New York, just too late for its hymns to be used in the new Episcopalian hymn book published that year. But perhaps it did not matter, and certainly not so far as this particular hymn was concerned, since American Episcopalians were content to wait until 1892 before including it among their authorized hymns. The hymn was included in *The* [Baptist] *Psalmist* of 1843 and *The Sabbath Hymn Book* [Congregational] of 1858, but, in the case of this, as of so many other hymns, the Boston Unitarians were the first to see its merits, and the only ones to make prompt use of it, which they did in 1830. It is to be remembered that the Orthodox churches at that date were satisfied to sing "Watts," or if they were to admit new hymns (enough to make "Watts and Select"), they preferred such new hymns as approached most closely to the old model.

Some years later Mr. Francis Arthur Jones attempted to trace the whereabouts of the original manuscript drafts of some of our popular hymns with a view to an article upon the subject in the *Strand Magazine*. He found that comparatively few such manuscripts have been preserved. In regard to those of Milman, his son, Mr. Arthur Milman, wrote: "I have never even seen a MS. Of my father, Dean Milman's hymns, and I greatly doubt whether any can have survived." It happened that Mr. Jones had secured an autograph of this hymn only two days prior to the receipt of Mr. Milman's letter, and from that the facsimile here reproduced was made. Concerning this he remarks: "Whether the MS. Is the original, or merely the 'fair' copy, I am unable to say. It came into my hands through a dealer, and I value it very highly.

THE AUTHOR OF THE HYMN

Henry Hart Milman, born February 10th, 1791, was the youngest child of Francis Milman, physician to George III, and created a baronet by that king. He was prepared for Oxford at Eton, and after a brilliant career took his degree at Brasenose College in 1813. Among the prizes he carried off was that for English poetry, an event chronicled in one of the Ingoldsby Legends:—

> "His lines on Apollo
> Beat all the rest hollow,
> And gained him the Newdigate prize."

While still at Oxford he wrote for his first drama, "Fazio: a Tragedy," published soon after his graduation. It was put upon the stage without his knowledge or consent, and acted with much success in England and America.

Ordained to the ministry in 1816, he became Vicar of St. Mary's Church, Reading. "He reads and preaches enchantingly," the famous Miss Mitford wrote soon after his coming; but he found in his parish some prejudice against him as the author of a play. He was full of industry and literary ambition, and followed in his drama with an epic poem in twelve books, "Samor, Lord of the Bright City." Then came three religious dramas which crowed his poetic career, the "Fall of Jerusalem" in 1820; the "Martyr of Antioch" and "Belshazzar," in 1822. For the copyright of each of these he received the large sum of five hundred guineas.

But with the last of the three the enthusiasm of critics and applause of the public, originally very great, had waned, and his later poems were not successful. All alike are now buried and forgotten. It seems strange, indeed, that a poet greeted with so much enthusiasm by his contemporaries should be remembered only by a few hymns. His poetical works, gathered into three comely volumes in 1839, and long out of print, contain much that is striking and beautiful; and not the least pleasing feature is their dedication "To her who has made the poetry of life reality, by her affectionate husband."

Milman was to win more permanent fame in another branch of literature. While still at Reading he published his *History of the Jews*, in which he attempted, for the first time in England, to read the sacred annals in the light of the principles of historical criticism. This effort brought down upon him a storm of indignation and abuse, for which, however, he was not unprepared, and which he weathered in silence. His later works, *The History of Christianity* and *The History of Latin Christianity*, placed him at once among the great historical writers of the language; and in that high place he remains. Promotion in the Church also came to him. In 1835 he was appointed rector of St. Margaret's, the church that stands in the shadow of Westminster Abbey; and in 1849 he became Dean of St. Paul's, the cathedral church of London.

Dean Milman's London life was one of incessant toil, and had its sorrows also, three of his children lying in one grave in the north aisle of the Abbey. He became a great figure in London, sought after for his social charm, admired for his learning and genius, and reverenced for his lofty and peculiarly straightforward Christian character. He was a liberal in theology, and stood resolutely apart from the High Church move-ment. He survived the full vigor of his mental powers until September 24th, 1868, and was buried in the crypt of his vast cathedral.

In 1900 appeared a biography of Dean Milman, by the son who has already been referred to. It had been delayed, strangely enough, until the generation of those who were his personal friends had passed away and the lustre of his poetic reputation had been dimmed by the lapse of time.

XXII

THINE FOR EVER! GOD OF LOVE

THE TEXT OF THE HYMN

1   Thine for ever! God of love,
    Hear us from Thy throne above;
    Thine for ever may we be
    Here and in eternity.

2   Thine for ever! Lord of life,
    Shield us through our earthly strife;
    Thou, the Life, the Truth, the Way
    Guide us to the realms of day.

3   Thine for ever! O how blest
    They who find in Thee their rest!
    Saviour, Guardian, heavenly Friend,
    O defend us to the end.

4   Thine for ever! Saviour, keep
    These Thy frail and trembling sheep;
    Safe alone beneath Thy care,
    Let us all thy goodness share.

5   Thine for ever! Thou our Guide,
    All our wants by Thee supplied,
    All our sins by Thee forgiven,
    Lead us, Lord, from earth to heaven.

Mary Fawler (Hooper) Maude, 1847

NOTE.–Five verses of the original seven. Some features of the text are referred to under "Some Points for Discussion."

THE STORY OF THE HYMN

A sensational or sentimental hymn may catch the ear of the public and at once gain a short-lived popularity. But a hymn of solid merit makes its way more slowly. It is not often that the writer of such a hymn lives to see it take its place in the permanent hymnody of the Church. Such, however, is the happy experience of Mrs. Maude, who wrote "Thine For Ever! God of Love." And it is certainly an additional happy circumstance that we now have the story of the hymn in her own words. Mrs. Maude has lately written it for the Rev. John Brownlie, as follows:—

"In 1847 my husband was minister of the Parish Church of St. Thomas, Newport, Isle of Wight. We had very large Sunday-schools, in which I taught the first class of elder girls, then preparing for their confirmation by the Bishop of Winchester. Health obliged me to go for some weeks to the seaside, and while there I wrote twelve letters to my class, which were afterward printed by the Church of England Sunday-School Institute. In one of the letters I wrote off, almost impromptu, the hymn *Thine for ever.*"

It should be explained, perhaps, that in the confirmation service in the Church of England the prayer spoken by the bishop in the act of laying on his hands begins, "Defend, O Lord, this thy Child with thy heavenly grace, that *he* may continue thine for ever." These words furnished the theme for the hymn. In the hymn they are taken up by catechumens and congregation, and made the words of their own prayer.

Mrs. Maude goes on to say: "The hymn must have been in some way seen by the committee of the Christian Knowledge Society, for early in the fifties I opened their newly-published hymnal, much to my surprise, upon my own hymn. After that, application for its use came in from all quarters. Little did I imagine that it would be chosen by our beloved Queen to be sung at the confirmation of a Royal Princess.

"It was our custom in Chirk Vicarage to sing a hymn, chosen in turn, at our evening family prayer on the Lord's Day. On Sunday, February 8th, 1887, it was my husband's turn to choose, and he gave out *Thine for ever,* looking round at me. On the 11th he was singing with saints in Paradise …

"Now, in my eightieth year, whenever I meet my hymn, there seems to be written across it, to my mental vision, *non nobis Domine.*"

Mrs. Maude's hymn is so admirably suited to a confirmation service that its early adoption in the Church of England can readily be understood. In this country the hymn does not seem to have been used in the Episcopal Church until 1872. By that time it was already getting to be familiar in such Presbyterian and Congregational churches as were using Dr. Robinson's *Songs for Sanctuary,* published in 1865.

In accounting for the wide use into which this hymn has come, one finds a reminder of the actual distinction between a collection of lyrical or even devotional poetry on the one hand and a hymn book on the other. If he were considering this hymn as a candidate for inclusion in a book of lyrics he would feel that it was lyrical in the sense of being eminently singable, but he would look in vain through its verses for any special structural beauty, for a thought or even a turn of expression that had anything of the charm of the unexpected. Nothing in it is far removed from the commonplace in a poetic sense. He might feel toward it much the same way, considered for a place even in a book of devotional poetry. He would recognize a real tenderness of feeling and a perfect refinement of expression. Why, even then, should it gain favor as against a vast body of verse as true in religious feeling and equally poetic, to say the least? But who, on the other hand, has ever heard Mrs. Maude's hymn sung heartily in connection with the act of admitting catechumens to the Table of their Lord without feeling something of the satisfaction that comes with the right word, to the occasion true because exactly expressive of the feeling which the occasion evokes? Mrs. Maude's verses, it would seem, find their proper place not in a book of poems, but in a service book. They are poetry in the sense of being liturgical verse, whose art consists in entering into the feelings of those participating in a certain service, and giving to them expression in perfect truth and in perfect taste. To bring out the poetry in them they must e sung, and sung in connection to the service they belong, and sung by those whose hearts respond to what the service means and stands for. There is abundant room for lyrics of high art in the hymn book, but there is also an inevitable demand for proper liturgical poetry.

In estimating the readiness of welcome which Mrs. Maude's hymn has found, one has also to remember that it did not have to make its way through a very formidable body of competitors. Even now it stands somewhat isolated on a bare spot of the domain of our hymnody. We have Bishop Wordsworth's conscientious and careful "Arm These Thy Soldiers, Mighty Lord" (*The Hymnal*, No. 315). But the hymn itself belongs to the Heavy Artillery, and rarely gets into active service. We also have President Davies's "Lord, I am Thine, Entirely Thine" (*The Hymnal*, No. 320), but many who have heard it sung by a great congregation must have felt that it should have remained rather as a secret between an individual soul and its Master. There are no other hymns for this occasion with the liturgical excellence of Mrs. Maude's. And that fact greatly strengthens its title to the place it now holds.

THE AUTHOR OF THE HYMN

Mary Fawler Hooper was born in 1819, and is the daughter of George H. Hooper, of Stanmore, Middlesex. In 1841 she was married to the Rev. Joseph Maude, who became Vicar of Chirk, in North Wales, and an Honorary Canon of St. Asaph's Cathedral, and whose death, in 1887, has been referred to already. In 1848 her *Twelve Letters on Confirmation* were published, and in 1852 she printed privately her *Memorials of Past Years*. She has written other hymns, mostly for use in her husband's parish, but none of these has come into general use.

Mrs. Maude's life has been in no sense that of a woman of letters, or one lived in the public eye. It has been that of the faithful wife of a village pastor, the sharer of his labors and his hopes. Of such a life, however successful, the rewards are not with men. Her hymn represents her one point of contact with the larger public. And even the hymn was written with no more ambitious aim than that of being helpful to a class of village girls. "The praise of any usefulness," Mrs. Maude modestly says in a recent letter, "must all be given to Him whose glory it is to work by such simple means." Mrs. Maude is now in the evening of her life, but it seems likely that for long her name will be pleasantly remembered in connection with the hymn of her younger days. (Mrs. Maude died in 1913.)

Printed in the United States
73939LV00003BA/1-174